MW00737428

Our Story

Book 1

The Blue Prints for Life

Shema

ISBN-13: 978-0615940120
ISBN-10: 0615940129
Visit us at thesoss.org or
Blueprint Publishing
thebluepritsforlife.org

DEDICATION

In loving memory of my daughter Victoria and my grandmother Eunice.

ACKNOWLEDGMENTS

This journey could not have been possible without my husband Hyde, the patience of my children Kris, Abby and Jacob and my mother Pamela.

It would have also been impossible without the digitized copies of ancient books by Google. Almost all of these books can be accessed online through Google's archives. I encourage the reader to download as many of these ancient books as you can. I must also acknowledge my friend Gerald Martin, for his insight.

Although I have written the information on paper, the story of our past was directed by the eternal and unsurpassing force of our universe.

Even the mystery which hath been hidden from ages and from generations, but now is made manifest to all.
Colossians 1:25-27
See for yourself the simplicity of all the mysteries of the world.

Contents

Introduction

When we go back in time, to trace Earth's history, one thing becomes apparent: *Our planet is alive,* she has a soul and a spirit, which has been here from the very beginning. We are like cells in her body and in every generation, some have been selected to record the events of their time. In this volume, we will tell the story of the Earth from records of those who have been employed from the generations to keep them.

The planet revolves around a global philosophy, it moves towards milestones, just like a growing being. These milestones are the philosophies which have shaped our sense of consciousness and purpose on Earth.

"America is therefore the land of the future, where, in the ages that lie before us, the burden of the World's History shall reveal itself." — Georg Wilhelm Friedrich Hegel

From the founding of this nation, the philosophy of *Justice and liberty for all,* steered the country and the world towards freedom, civil rights, equality and ending slavery. But in the 19th century, those who lost the fight to maintain segregation and slavery, invented a new philosophy, *survival of the fittest. This philosophy* discarded ancient records like the bible and gradually incited the highest perversion of capitalism and passive racism. History was for the first time being rewritten by the losers, who were determined to win the war somewhere else.

But there was a subtle outcry for more evidence, those considered weak and unfit demanded a new philosophy. They elected for change once again. Their cries reached heaven and the response is our new philosophy: *the meek will inherit the Earth.* (Psalm 37:11, Matthew 5:5)

If the Earth has been left to the meek, then there must be a deed somewhere with our names on the title. We are like wealthy royals who have been robbed and left stranded on Earth. Our robbers were generous enough to give many treasures back, but the most valuable treasure of all, is our memory. We now live in our mansions, but as servants barred from the master's chamber and the robbers as our masters. The masons who built these mansions have left us many clues; so the goal of this course is to discover the clues which they have left behind.

This philosophy is our mandate to discover the truth, and it is so simple that within a few pages you will discover where you are in history, as you trace the footprints of your ancestors, through science and art. You will read a thousand words from each image; as the ancient archives speak for themselves. This volume concentrates on the journey we have all taken to get here. It can only be equated to following a treasure map; except our map is the bible and the treasure is our collective memory of who we really are.

[1]History is unlike any other subject, in that our knowledge of it must come to us wholly through indirect means. All our information regarding the past has to be obtained in one form or another through other people; so in seeking a trustworthy description of Charlemagne, the proper course would be to lay hold first of whatever evidence has come down directly from Charlemagne's day to our own, and to put larger trust in this than in more recent accounts which have been played upon by the imagination of their authors and perhaps rendered wholly misleading by errors consciously or unconsciously injected into them.

It is easy to get carried away with our paint brush and to paint the faces of the ancients more like ourselves; because we were there in some form, so their history is rightfully ours.

But for fear of propagating the blank spaces with prejudice, we must become like literary archaeologists, literally digging through the archives of the ancient historians and ethnographers. We must hand them the paint brush and the pen and simply observe ourselves as we were then. It is not enough to restate Herodotus' opinions or to quote a snippet of Lucians' story. We must also examine the context of their story. We must examine the possible cultural and political correctness of the environment, in which they are trying to convey this information. Who else is there and what do they see? What are they trying to preserve? And why do they feel the urgency to preserve it? Is there a message encrypted for future generations?

When this is done, what you exhume will baffle you. When all the fragments are reconnected, the story they tell is so incredible, and the images in the mosaic are so unsettling, that I have copied their words like the images verbatim.

Now with one voice emanating from a singular source, all the generations of mankind, join me to tell our story.

My name is Shema, and I was born to tell this story, to follow this map and to unearth the most valuable treasure to all of humanity. My name in Hebrew means *"God is One"* and as the story goes he is in everything and nothing goes against his purpose. In everything he remains one; with one history, purpose, one science and a unity of form.

It does not matter what you believe, it only matters what is true. What you believe may be false, but what is true can be proven. If what you believe is true, then you should not be afraid to test it. Let us follow the pioneers of science and philosophy who have given us the foundation of all our knowledge of the world. These prophets will reveal this final philosophy in the synthesis of science and theology.

We return to the era of the Egyptians where the integration of science and philosophy was magic; and the sons of God spoke to their environment.

---

[1] A source book of mediæval history: documents illustrative of European life and institutions from the German invasion to the renaissance by Frederic Austin Ogg/ American Book Company, 1907

FOR TRUTH

He set his battle in array, and thought
To carry all before him, since he fought
For Truth, whose likeness was to him revealed;
Whose claim he blazoned on his battle-shield;
But found in front, impassively opposed,
The World against him, with its ranks all closed:

He fought, he fell, he failed to win the day
But led to Victory another way.

For Truth, it seemed, in very person came
And took his hand, and they two in one flame
Of dawn, directly through the darkness passed;
Her breath far mightier than the battle-blast.
And here and there men caught a glimpse of grace,
A moment's flash of her immortal face,
And turned to follow, till the battle-ground
Transformed with foemen slowly facing round
To fight for Truth, so lately held accursed,
As if they had been her champion from the first.
Only a change of front, and he who had led were left behind with Her forgotten dead.

By Gerald Massey

The Journey to Truth

When I began this journey to tell the story of our time here on Earth, I was still a seven year old girl growing up on the island of St. Lucia. There was no gold or silver, nothing besides the natural pyramids; but the French and English fought fourteen brutal wars to lay claim to what they called the *Helen of the West*.

Figure 1 Pyramid like peaks on the south-eastern part of the island of St.Lucia

Just a few centuries ago my grandmother says, that young people were brought here from Africa. They must have come from different regions, because they had to develop a brand new language to communicate with each other. An amalgamation of dialects like Latin, French, English, and some African called Patios. While most of the world advanced, St. Lucia was still very young; and its umbilical connection to England was only severed a few hours after I was born at the end of 1978.

Most Saint Lucians aren't aware of the origins of their culture; but culture and tradition also give insight as to where we have been in the past. St. Lucians celebrate festivals like La Rose and La Marguerite, which are believed to have stemmed from the ancient Rosicrucian order and from Freemasonry. Our oral traditions reinforced a sense of community and a very primitive bound to our ancestors. They came over to the west most as teenagers without any inheritance or token from the past. They had nothing but their story; and these stories were so significant, that generations later we kept the stories; because it was all that was left of them. Through these stories we were constantly reminded that we did not have an independent identity. There was no I. The ancients transmitted their souls, their unfinished goals, and unanswered questions through their stories. Grooming one of us to replace each runner of the long relay, and receive their baton as they ended their race.

Since electricity and telecommunications eluded us, time stood still and progress slow; but these oral traditions on dark stormy nights prevailed.

When I grew up, I found myself telling these very same stories to my children and I began to wonder where they came from. Stories of magic doors to other places in the world, and of men crossing over the symbolic bridges which led them there, mysterious structures erected overnight, burglars trapped in the houses they entered and some all too real events which confirmed them. But what started this journey at age seven was a simple dream. I remember that day as vivid as if it were yesterday.

It was about six o'clock in the morning, when the sound of the cocks crowing in the back yard, awakened me to the dawn of a new day. My grandmother was brewing fresh Caribbean coffee, and the aroma forced me out of bed. Around the kitchen table which looked more like a bar, my aunts Lindy and Linda and my mom began the family tradition of relaying their dreams from the night before.

They believed that their dreams later came true, and on this morning as my mother begun to tell us what she dreamt, something strange happened. There was a knock at the door, it was our neighbor miss Fortuna; my mother continued uninterrupted as miss Fortuna's jaw dropped in shock; "What's wrong?" my grandmother asks in Creole. "I was just coming to tell y' all about Mr. Fred's accident up on the hill," she replied. It turned out that my mother's dream was a description of the accident just as it happened. Everyone's expression was the type of elation, like watching a baby take its first steps or say its first words. But I was so intrigued that I began to question how this was even possible.

The grownups around me took it for granted that their dreams peaked into the future. They were psychics' each day revealing a glimpse of a day to come. What did that mean? Could we have prevented Mr. Fred's accident? This was my awakening. From that day on I began searching for the answers of life. My grandmother Eunice, was a deeply religious Christian and the bible was her most prized possession. When she was a young girl the Catholic priests prohibited the reading of the bible. Magic and voodoo were also labelled as evil and strictly prohibited; so as a child in an advanced world she naturally became very curious. This curiosity sparked the belief that our secrets were guarded in this book. The book was alive and within it, were all the words which God had ever spoken, is speaking or will speak. So I gathered the scattered pieces and compared the stories.

When I immigrated into the US, I realized that the quest for truth was embodied in my name, Sherma. East Indians thought that I was Sharma, and with the maiden name Albertini and my anomalous red hair, some guessed I had a European background. But when I was reborn, I lost the "r" in my name and finally understood how all of our stories were synthesized.

The most astounding discovery, was that their superstition that our secrets had been recorded in the book was real. This truth was known in the deepest parts of us, because our ancestors embedded a genetic copy of their stories in our DNA. Although some of us have had parts of the story genetically and literally deleted or altered; when we combine the African, Arabian, Asian, Indian, European and the Jew, all the missing pieces fit together. This speaks volumes for our place in history, because now that we are united, we can finally see with the All Seeing Eye. All of our backgrounds and perspectives allows us to see the truth completely; and the truth shall set us free.

I have read all the books that we were forbidden to read and eaten the fruits which we were forbidden to eat. I asked and received and knocked and a new door opened. Before me was truth, in all its simplicity. A familiar spirit was commanding things to be and telling the story from the beginning. Only now, I could understand the language.

We have come a long way, we have all crossed many barriers to find it, but here it was the most powerful force in all the universe; and a little girl from a tiny island was here in its presence. Amazed and astounded, that the place where I was standing was the end of our story.

The Foundation of Ideology and Religion

As we trace our development through the evolution of our guiding Spirit, we discover the prevailing themes which endure. Like any story, our story and history unfolds with plots and twists, through elements and allegories throughout the story. There are an infinite number of events captured within each era; but once we follow the tracks of our divine guide, we can see events unfold in perfect sequence.

In an old Indian tale of six blind men describing an elephant. Each man holding on to a piece of the elephant describes it as he feels. The man holding the trunk, thinks that the elephant is like a giant snake, while the one feeling the body envisions a great wall. The man who can see the entire animal, then explains how they were all wrong, yet they were all-together right. So it is with the history of the Earth, it has been told from many angles; and almost always underlining the very narrow perspective of the story teller. It essentially becomes his-story and not necessarily a complete and accurate account of our past. The one who is to convince us that the elephant is a giant snake must drown out the voices of all the other men; but to determine the truth we must seek a synthesis. Thankfully the one who can see the entire elephant, can direct us all to the missing pieces of the story.

If we were created by the same force then all of our stories are relevant; but the bible has been preserved as the most reliable medium we can use to translate all of these stories.

Science confirms that we are all one people from one couple, *Adam and Eve*. We are different because of the roles we must play, but joined in the pursuit of life. We are locked into states which confine and define us; like race, religion, nationality, political affiliations and educational backgrounds. These boxes allow us a particular perspective in the development of truth, but are only a small portion of it. The fact is religion and race, were created to divide us. Like the biological process of differentiation which brings to life one being. Division is just one of the things which we have been socialized to create. Almost all religion search for absolute truth with the exclusion of external concepts.

True love and the absolute spirit, is only discovered, when we remove the barriers of division which perpetuate the confusion instituted among us. When we follow the trail of the infinite spirit of the Earth, we can finally begin to see our stories in harmony.

[2]History affirms evidence of German philosopher G.W.F Hegel's dialectic process. Hegel believed that ultimate truth or the *Absolute Spirit* was being developed throughout history. A

---

[2]Times 100 ideas that changed the world. Hegel Outlines the Dialectic pg. 78 G.W.F. Hegel 1770-1831

thesis or idea would eventually develop its antithesis, the opposite of the original idea. Eventually the opposing ideas would be reconciled in a synthesis and the process would begin again. This is what we observe in history. Like strands of DNA history repeats itself so that what we see in one form today will reverse tomorrow, keeping the basic essence of the story. The hour glass must turn over, the pendulum must return, even the poles will flip. Everything resets when one end reaches its climax. It collapses under its gravity and from its ashes emerges the building blocks of the other. Without these extremes, there would be no change or growth or even time. This is the story of life, a process of revolving cycles, recycled stories with the same themes; and not evolving transformations. The jest of our story, is how the roles reverse through time. The wise become fools, kings become slaves, the destitute become princes, destroyers become builders and builders become destroyers.

Science illuminates these stories by providing the genetic, archeological and forensic interpretations. In a sense we are combing through the ancient stories with a scientific lens. Our story unfolds through six symbols, the great serpent, the elephant and cattle, (including a giraffe, horse, or donkey) but the main characters are the external force, the man and the woman.

These symbols always mark a point on the journey, they become like pons in a chess game. The serpent signifies wisdom while the woman represents the transition or acquisition of it. The elephant represents a type of Nirvana, a position which avoids the cycles of growth and death. This is the symbol of eternal life which was barred from man and is not represented in the bible at all. The cattle (horse, donkey or Giraffe) signifies the seizing of power as it runs ahead into a new Era. It implies a new period of enlightenment, perspective or direction. This may be the ancient reasoning for the horse shoe as an omen of good luck. The man, is the rider, a general, a king or prophetic leader which a nation or people must follow. In the US. "The man," is a *street* synonym for the system of authority and government. The end of the story begins always with the woman and the beginning of a new era begins when she gives birth to a new man.

The cultures which seek nirvana embrace the elephant; but must limit the birth and development of the woman to avoid these cycles, while other cultures exalt her ability to wield the mighty serpent.

The accuracy and consistency of these symbols and themes is astounding. Every portion of the story has been thoroughly researched and fortified with immense geographic, genetic and scientific as well as photographic evidence. This permits us to read the bible as scientists and historians with the understanding that the records of our past were inspired by the superior intelligence which has directed man throughout this journey.

A study of the origin and history of the bible, indicates that there are traditions which predate its incorporation. These stories help illuminate the actual historical settings of the bible; so that the oral traditions of the indigenous people suddenly become more enlightening.

Then when we piece all the fragmented stories together we arrive at the original story. Our story, the whole elephant, ears, trunk, feet, and all. Now let's get to the beginning.

In The Beginning

Genesis through Exodus gives us the earliest account of our history; but it is not written as a day by day expose of life in the beginning. It is a record of the *significant* milestones which mark our evolution through time.

This is the story about the creation of humans and the Garden of Eden which was specifically designed for us, within a long established and volatile Earth.

Genesis 2

1 Thus the heavens and the earth were finished, and all the host of them.

2 And on the seventh day God ended his work which he had made; and he rested

Before Eden

Life is defined by heat, movement and growth; so as the author of life, when God declares a rest from all work, this coincides with the last Glacial Maximum. Scientists say that this period Lasted from approximately 110,000 to 10,000 years ago. During this ice age much more of the Earth was cold, dry, dusty and uninhabitable. The dust levels were as much as 20 to 25 times greater than they are today. There was also little vegetation, or precipitation to clear dust from the atmosphere; but temperatures raised and the icy ground begun to melt, and this process prepared a home for man.

4 These are the generations of the heavens and of the earth when they were created,

5 And every plant of the field before it was in the earth, and every herb of the field before it grew: for the Lord God had not caused it to rain upon the earth, and there was not a man to till the ground.

6 But there went up a mist from the earth, and watered the whole face of the ground.

7 And the Lord God formed man out of all the dust, and breathed into his nostrils the breath of life; and man became a living soul.

*8 And the Lord God planted a garden **eastward in Eden; and there he put the man whom he had formed**.*

Location of Eden

*10 And a river went out of Eden to water the garden; and from thence it was parted, and became into **four heads**.*

11 The name of the first is Pison: which compasseth the whole land of Havilah, where there is gold;

12 And the gold of that land is good: there is bdellium and the onyx stone.

*13 And the name of the second river is Gihon: the same is it that compasseth the whole land of **Ethiopia**.*

*14 And the name of the third river is Hiddekel: which goeth toward the east of **Assyria**. And the fourth river is Euphrates.*

The coordinates for Eden's location send us to the North of Ethiopia (but not true North because we must pass through a land filled with ancient gold mines, like ancient Nubia now Sudan) then we stop to the

West of Assyria (Assyria was located in northwestern Iraq on the right bank of the Tigris River), with the Mediterranean boundary to the North. Eden must have encompassed the Sahara region towards Egypt. Scientists say that about 10,500 years ago the Sahara became a tropical paradise and according to the bible this was our Eden.

The biblical summary of how Eden was created seems simple, but it is extremely technical. The Saharan rains were not caused by falling water from heavy condensed clouds in the sky; but from the evaporation and *rising* of warm air over land and oceans.

A *mist* *went up* to water the ground, this describes monsoon rains.

When Adam and Eve may have occupied this garden seems to be about 11 thousand years ago. When *the Lord God took the man, and put him into the garden of Eden Gen 2:9* and Gen 2:15.

The fossil records to date suggest that man was actually formed further South in Ethiopia, where the oldest fossils of humans have been discovered.

Diodorus Siculus was an ancient Sicilian Ethnographer/historian and the author of *the history of the universe Bibliotheca historica* from 60 to 30 BC. In (book 1 page 151-152) he related that

The Ethiopians say, that they were the first men that ever were in the world; and that the Egyptians are a colony drawn out from them by Osiris; and that Egypt was formerly no part of the continent, but a sea, at the beginning of the world.;

How long was man formed before Eden, can be debated between the Ethiopian records of over 23,000 years and the scientific calculations of more than 70,000. Scientists say that the genes of our earliest male ancestor are about [3]70,000 years old. But when Adam moved into Eden seems to be restricted to the beginning of the Tropical Sahara 10,500 years ago. [4]For now we will synchronize our genetic evolution with our historical development (70,000/10,416 = 6.72) and this leaves us with a factor of 6.72 years. It is obvious that there was time long before Eden, but it seems that all that we can detect from this period are fragments of tools and bones. There is no evidence of civilization, or anything crucial to the evolution of human cognition. For this reason the bible begins Our Story in Eden.

So we will also start here within this Absolute time frame of 10, 416 years ago.

Eve was the first person to be created from flesh and blood (Genesis 2:23) and the mother of the only surviving species of Man the children of Adam, wise men, or Homo sapiens Genesis 3:20. Before their transformation into wise men or Homo sapiens, we are told that they were able to communicate with animals. Then after *their eyes open*ed, they recognized that they were naked, and their need for clothing was sparked.

The divine pushed them through many experiences of loss, tragedy and transformation on the journey to realize this new found wisdom. As they graduated from one comfort zone to another, they learnt new lessons about the world they would later control.

The first lesson came from the loss of Eden where Genesis 3: 22-24 characterized the desertification of the Sahara as a *flaming sword. And the Lord God said:*

Behold, the man is become as one of us, to know good and evil: [so God defines himself as one with infinite knowledge] *and now, lest he put forth his hand, and take also of the tree of life, and eat, and live forever:*

---

[3] The age of Adam as determined by National Geographic Explorer Spencer Wells in Journey to Man.
[4] See end notes under "Additional Resources," for The Age of Adam.

Therefore the Lord God sent him forth from the garden of Eden, to till the ground from whence he was taken. So he drove out the man; and he placed at the east of the garden of Eden Cherubims, and a flaming sword which turned every way, to keep the way of the tree of life.

The loss of their perfect Eden also pushed them further and further towards the [5]East. This push led to the transition out of Eden and eventually out of Africa. Cain left the family very early on, moving away from the *face of God,* which has been superficially outlined as Chad of central Africa. His tribe is credited with the first city ever built, equipped with musical instruments and advance metallurgy. This may refer to the early Natufian and Göbekli Tepe civilizations, to the east of Egypt in the Levant region extending from Israel to Southern Turkey.

*17 And Cain knew his wife; and she conceived, and bare Enoch: and he builded a city, and called the name of the **city,** after the name of his son, Enoch.*
18 And unto Enoch was born Irad:
21 And his brother's name was Jubal: he was the father of all **such as handle the harp and organ**.
*22 And Zillah, she also bare Tubalcain, an instructor of every artificer in **brass and iron**: and the sister of Tubalcain was Naamah. Gen 4:17-22*

Adam and the generations which preceded Noah, form Haplogroups A and B in genetics. They remained in Africa and moved South and Westward from the Sahara. When Adam finally exited Eden, is unclear but it is believed that by 4000 B.C. or roughly 6000 years ago, the Sahara was entirely vacated and these families dispersed throughout the continent. Those who held on to Eden's final frontier settled in Egypt and raised the platforms of the most enduring civilization of all time. Some skirted the Libyan part, *north* of the Sahara where their drawings on rocks illustrate the cries for rain and the reluctance of people to leave their utopian home.

Eviction from Eden

---

[5] Many of the cardinal points of direction mentioned in Genesis e.g. North/South are in relation to the Sahara desert.

Adam

6 *Figure 2 Drawings of cattle in a cave, two San men, huge python snake shaped rock.*

Adam may have resembled the South African **San/Saan or** [7]*Khoi-Khoi (which means the first men).* They say that they were the first inhabitants of the world, making them the direct descendants of Adam; and their DNA actually confirms this. Their copper complexion is lighter than many imagine as indigenous of Africans; but it is easy to visualize how the Asians, Caucasians, and Arabians came from them.

Scientists discovered thousands of paintings in a cave called the *Mountain of the Gods,* and a large snake-carved rock (*above right*) which means that these were the first masons. Their stories of our beginning draws on the metaphors and mythical images of the Elephant, Giraffe and the *mighty Serpent*, the great trickster able to assume any form. Their early stage of development provides a tiny glimpse of the world through the developing consciousness.

Without the distractions of our day, a powerful force communicated telepathically and they developed an interconnected intuition with their world. They know that their livestock is nearing extinction and feel the declining rain and the drought coming. They are gradually nudged from one place to the next, always trusting that the new home would be safe, and food would be plenty. The force about them obliges, and prepares a home for them driving every threat into extinction before they arrive. They understood that our system was voice activated and owned the voice to command things into existence. Magic and Voodoo developed as cries of an infant to the ears of mother Earth.

[8]*Voodoo practitioners believe in one god, but they communicate with the divine through thousands of spirits, or "Loa," which have power over nature and human existence. The souls of the deceased act as intermediaries between God and the living. The individual not only has direct access to the spirit world, he or she actually becomes the god themselves."*

The dead were alive through them. They carried on in the flesh while their ancestors guided them in spirit. Miniature Gods like the voodoo Gods of West Africa and the ancient customs found in Ghana have been connected to the ancient Hellenes of Mycenae and Minoa in Greece.

---

[6] *Sheila Coulson, Sigrid Staurset, and Nick Walker (2011) "Ritualized Behavior in the Middle Stone Age: Evidence from Rhino Cave, Tsodilo Hills, Botswana" PaleoAnthropology 2011:18-61*

[7] The Natural Genesis: Or, Second Part of A Book of the Beginnings, Containing an Attempt to Recover and Reconstitute the Lost Origines of the Myths and Mysteries, Types and Symbols, Religion and Language, with Egypt for the Mouthpiece and Africa as the Birthplace, Volume 1Gerald Massey Williams and Norgate, 1883 pg. 115

[8]Anthropologist Wade Davis, a National Geographic Explorer-in-Residence who has studied voodoo extensively in Haiti.

⁹*The archaeological discoveries show a long history of Minoan contact* (settlement) *by black and African cultures from the very beginnings of early Minoan civilization.*

10*Many scholars take the Mycenaean's to be Minoans who established themselves on the mainland of Greece. Pg. 21*
Minoan art, was taken over wholly and without change by the Mycenaean's. Pg. 32
Mycenaean gems show very often a man struggling with a lion or a bull. A similar custom is found in Central Africa among the Beli, when a young man has killed a lion, a leopard or an elephant.

Noah's lineage developed the genetic marker M168 identified among the settlers east of the Sahara in present-day Ethiopia, Kenya, and Tanzania. This is the head of three branches which all the people outside of Africa stem from; but also includes most Africans. Before the age of genetic testing, it was assumed that East Africans represented an admixture of European ancestry.

11In Greek, Ethiopian referred to all people of very dark skin but the *European name for the Ethiopians was an Arabic word, signifying a "mixed race." On which account the natives scornfully disclaim it.*

Geneticists have discovered that **12** *The fact that the Ethiopians and Somalis have a subset of the sub-Saharan African haplotype diversity—and that the non-African populations have a subset of the diversity present in Ethiopians and Somalis—makes simple-admixture models less likely; rather, these observations support the hypothesis that a subset of this northeastern-African population* <u>*migrated out of Africa and populated the rest of the globe.*</u>

---

⁹ Race and the Writing of History : Riddling the Sphinx: Maghan Keita Assistant Professor of History and Director of Africana Studies Villanova University Social Science -Oxford University Press, 2000
¹⁰ The Mycenaean Origin of Greek Mythology by Martin Persson Nilsson University of California Press, Jan 1, 1972
¹¹ Nubia and Abyssinia: comprehending their civil history, antiquities, arts, religion, literature, and natural history Michael Russell, J. & J. Harper, 1833 – Ethiopia
¹²(Tishkoff et al. 1996a, 1998a, 1998b; Calafell et al. 1998; Kidd et al. 1998)

The biblical journey now zooms in on the path which led to civilization outside of Africa, and away from the *face of God*. On this path Noah and his three sons, take us through the rest of this journey. They retreated further east and may have met up with the descendants of Cain who had run from Eden years earlier. These generations built ancient empires on the fringes of Eden in Assyria. But as temperatures continued to rise, it produced a chain of events, like melting glaciers, earthquakes, volcanic eruptions and tsunamis.

Submerged settlements like Atlit-Yam on the coast of Israel were covered by rising sea-levels probably from a volcanic collapse of Mount Etna. Then a 10-storey tsunami engulfed the Mediterranean coast within hours about [13]8,000 years ago.

[14]*The village was destroyed, ~8.3 KY B.P., by a tsunami triggered by a known Holocene flank collapse of Mt. Etna volcano (Italy).*

Then around the same time, (6100 BC) or 8000 years ago, [15]three Storegga landmasses in the Norwegian Sea, at the edge of Norway's continental shelf broke off. This caused a catastrophic flooding of Doggerland by one of the largest tsunamis in recent history (up to 20 meters (66 ft.) high in the North Atlantic Ocean. These tsunamis led to a dramatic rise in worldwide sea levels and were powerful enough to brake off Britain from the mainland European continent. *Genesis 7:11 the fountains of the deep were broken (*the deep refers to the oceans).

In 1996 marine geologists, William B.F. Ryan and Walter C. Pitman from Columbia University found even more evidence for the flood.

According to the National Geographic, it *funneled through the narrow Bosporus, the water hit the Black Sea with 200 times the force of Niagara Falls. Each day the Black Sea rose about six inches (15 centimeters), and coastal farms were flooded.*

[16]Explorer Robert Ballard, who discovered the *Titanic,* discovered yet another part of our story. Ballard and his research team found the remains of abundant wooden beams which show signs of having been worked on by tools. Ballard believes that it represents an ancient structure that was apparently flooded in a deluge of biblical proportions off the coast of northern Turkey, 311 feet (95 meters) below the Black Sea. These beams may be evidence of the huge ark.

Genesis 8:4 says that Noah and his three sons (Japheth, Ham and Shem) were instructed to build an Ark to save them and the land animals from this flood. The ark may have also allowed for a final selection of

---

[13] The dates calculated by scientists seem to be much greater than the time estimated by the bible, but the only discrepancy is time. The flood itself cannot be not debated.

[14] Geophysical Research Letters, Volume 34, Issue 16, CiteID L16317 08/2007
Holocene tsunamis from Mount Etna and the fate of Israeli Neolithic communities by
Pareschi, Maria Teresa; Boschi, Enzo; Favalli, Massimiliano of AA(Istituto Nazionale di Geofisica e Vulcanologia, Pisa, Italy), AB(Istituto Nazionale di Geofisica e Vulcanologia, Pisa, Italy), AC(Istituto Nazionale di Geofisica e Vulcanologia, Pisa, Italy) 10.1029/2007GL030717 2007GeoRL..3416317P

[15] Bondevik, Stein; Dawson, Sue; Dawson, Alastair; Lohne, Øystein (5 August 2003). "Record-breaking Height for 8000-Year-Old Tsunami in the North Atlantic". EOS, Transactions of the American Geophysical Union 84 (31): 289, 293. Bibcode:2003EOSTr..84..289B. doi:10.1029/2003EO310001.

[16] http://www.ncdc.noaa.gov/paleo/ctl/clihis10k.html

humans and the domestication of animals. Those who were obedient, followed the directions, and avoided the greatest catastrophe of our time.

[17]According to the natives, (of Bornu, Central Africa) the true name is Barr Noa, or "Land of Noah". Then the legend seizing on this word, related that here the ark settled after the subsidence of the waters, the African Ararat being sought in the isolated Hajar Teus rock, on the south side of lake Tsad.

Ancient historians noted the African continent was overrun with wild beast as it is to this day. This eliminates Africa as the place of the ark's descent.

Jeremiah says that the sand of the Sahara was actually placed as a barrier for the waters of the flood; so that some of the generations from Adam, like the **San**, may have been preserved, but are not mentioned because their descendants are not represented outside of Africa at all. The ark represents the bottleneck of all the people outside of Africa.

Fear ye not me? saith the Lord: will ye not tremble at my presence, which have placed the sand for the bound of the sea by a perpetual decree, that it cannot pass it: and though the waves thereof toss themselves, yet can they not prevail; though they roar, yet can they not pass over it? Jeremiah 5:22

This sand also filtered the receding waters from the ocean, leaving salt mines in the Sahara and the Dead Sea Lake in Jerusalem, where merchants have harvested most of the salt of the Earth.

Sand is still a symbol used in black magic, as a spiritual wall or fence against an enemy.

[18]The ark rested in Armenia It is said, there is still some part of this ship in Armenia, at the mountain of Cordyaens; and that some people carry off pieces of the bitumen, which they use chiefly as amulets, for the averting of mischiefs.

The map also provides a few clues which confirm that Armenia is actually the "Place of Descent". First when the dove is freed from the Ark the leaf which it brings back to Noah is from an olive tree. This helps to narrow the search, to the Middle Eastern region where the only indigenous olives originated apart from the Sahara.

The second clue is found in Genesis 9:20-21

And Noah began to be a husbandman, and he planted a vineyard: And he drank of the wine, and was drunken. Agriculture is also believed to have been spawned here, making Noah the pioneer of this Neolithic Revolution. Then the oldest winery on Earth was discovered in Armenia in the region of Northern Iraq. Studies of the many varieties of grapes have shown that this is most likely to be their origin. Armenia was also a second type of Eden, endowed with a rich supply of grapes, whole grains and olive oil, which are foods found in a Mediterranean diet. Jesus completes the recipe with fish. These are also mentioned throughout the bible in conjunction with longevity.

---

[17] The Earth and Its Inhabitants ...: West Africa Elisée Reclus, Ernest George Ravenstein, Augustus Henry Keane D. Appleton, 1892 pg. 360

[18] The Complete Works of Flavius-Josephus the Celebrated Jewish Historian by William Whiston 1895 Book 1 chp 3

Once the ark landed, the residents dispersed to build new civilizations, and scaffolds of ancient civilizations begun to go up. But Noah's oldest son Japheth and his family were so traumatized by the flood that they decide never to build any settlement ever again. They were first to separate from the extended family; carrying the terror and the legend of the flood to distant cultures around the world.

Japheth formed the first branch Haplogroup C-M130, ~~45,000~~/ 6696 years ago. This is the Malayo-Polynesian family of languages, spoken by 385.5 million Austronesian people, of the *island* nations of Southeast Asia and the Pacific Ocean. These include many groups from the Aborigines to native Hawaiians; and are characterized as "Negritos" many with straighter hair, than Negros but also dark skinned.

By these were the <u>islands</u> *of the Gentiles divided in their lands; every-one after his tongue, after their families, in their nations*. Genesis 10:5 Japheth's descendants are depicted as *islanders* who dwell in tents. Genesis 9:27

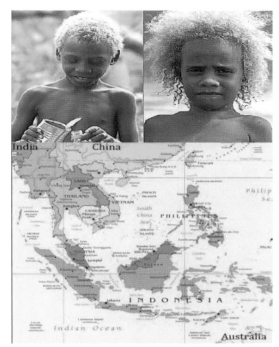

Figure 4 a).Vanuatu boy from Melanesia 2. Vanuatu girl. By Graham Crumb

[19]On December 26th, 2004 a tsunami hit the Indian Ocean. Seismologists had not prepared people for this disaster so it claimed the lives of thousands; but the small Moken tribe in Thailand, remembered the signs and were saved because *"they knew it was coming."* One of the elders said that *the great spirit of the sea purges periodically*. All the animals and just this one tribe understood the coming danger.

Noah's grandsons from his second son Ham, returned to try to find Eden again; but his great-grandson, Nimrod son of Cush remained in the Armenian region.

Figure 3 Papuans on the Lorentz River in Western New Guinea in 1912-13 Tropenmuseum by Prof. A.A. (August Adriaan) Pulle (photographer).Potisuwan

And Kush begat Nimrod: <u>*he began to be*</u> *a mighty one in the earth. And the beginning of his kingdom was Babel, and Erech, and Accad, and Calneh, in the land of Shinar.* This is the Mesopotamian Region around the Black Sea.

---

[19]http://www.cbsnews.com/stories/2005/03/18/60minutes/main681558.shtml

Out of that land went forth Asshur, and builded Nineveh, and the city Rehoboth, and Calah, and Resen between Nineveh and Calah: the same is a great city. Genesis 10:8-10

Figure 5 a). Coronus-(city-settlement of the Indus Valley Civilization) b).Grjatoi- (Indus Valley Civilization) c). Copper Dancing Girl d). Sculpture of a Priest/King. Image by Mammon Mengal-world66.com Afghan President Hamid Karzai in 2004

Nimrod became the founder of the genetic marker E-(M9) of those who remained in the region of Turkey, Armenia and Georgia; and dispersed to form various races around the world. The descendants of Shem also remained in this area and may have mixed with those of Nimrod.

The earliest historical records for a civilization after the flood, date around 3500 BC or 5500 years ago. "*Babel*" may have been the point when the populations finally recovered from complete obliteration. These survivors developed agriculture and had greater control over their food supply. The growing populations, gave birth to a more complex social organization, and sparked the need for trade, the development of writing, methods of calculating time, and defined laws relative to worship and general co-existence. This rapid growth led to our separations into diverse races and civilizations, at a time when many towers were being erected throughout the Earth. This division is represented geographically, linguistically as well as physically, as men begun to multiply separately. Noah's other son Ham migrated back to Africa, probably in search of Eden. He gave birth to Canaan, Egypt, Nubia/Cush and the East African civilizations. The son of Cush or Ethiopia, Nimrod (M9), gave birth to 90 percent of the people outside of the African continent. *Genesis 10:8-10*

So to the question: can the Ethiopian change his skin color? Jeremiah 13:23 the answer is a resounding yes. But even about the 5th century BC the Father of History, Herodotus one of the most cited ancient historians and our very first Ethnographer (484 – 425 BC) described the people of the region, very similar to their ancient founder:

As for me, I judge the Colchis's (Turks, Armenians and Georgians*) to be a colony of the Egyptians, because like them, they are black with woolly hair.*

One of these premiere ancient civilizations was called Mohenjo-Daro, illustrated above. It extended over 1,260,000 km², making it the largest of ancient civilizations. This very advanced empire is believed to have existed from 3000 until 1600 BC in the Indus Valley beneath the Hindu Kush ranges in present-day Pakistan northwest India.

At this point Genesis 11:1 explains that all the earth had one *language* and common words. [20]In Hebrew this literally means one *lip* or feature and common *words* may refer to their genetic information

---

[20] NAS Exhaustive Concordance of the Bible with Hebrew-Aramaic and Greek Dictionaries by The Lockman Foundation

and what these words spelled in terms of race. Language also provides genetic and archaeological evidence, which scientists use to trace our migration patterns; so that population relationships can be predicted on the basis of common ancestry as well as on the basis of geographic and linguistic similarity.

To create separate races or confound the languages, humans needed to be separated into various groups. Their common founders, diets, micro-organic epidemics or plagues and (not climatological adaptations) led to our very recent racial distinctions. For this reason the biblical record of our journey throughout the Earth is illustrated through the development of various languages as they correspond to these races.

The number of new immigrants, to an area can be measured by the degree to which a language changes or is entirely replaced.

Some scientists say that: [21]*it is likely that most of the diversity we see now, already existed in the ancestral African population.*

The traits which seem to define particular races were already part of the distinctions among the ancient population. Thus we find a wide variety of traits among Africans, which are similar to all of the other races.

[22]*A new report on the evolution of a gene for skin color suggested that Europeans acquired pale skin quite recently, only 5300 to 6000 years ago.* This new dating matches the division from the tower almost precisely at 3000BC.

Also human races seem to have very recent origins. For the most part, physical traits that distinguish modern human geographic groups only appear in the fossil record within the past ~~30~~/ 4464 years. (That's only 2400 years BC)

Geneticist have [23]*found that compared to African Americans, European-American populations had a higher proportion of potentially harmful mutations. There are "400 mutations per individual that are possibly deleterious [or damaging]" the individuals studied carry several hundred mutations that likely disrupt protein function."*

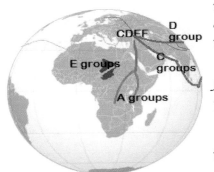

Finally the differences can most likely be attributed to *fragmentation of human groups-not hundreds of thousands of years of separate evolution.*

These fragments then went on to reproduce the specific traits of their founder, which became more pronounced through social selection pressures.

*Figure 6 The ancestral population from **Noah**, through his sons, Shem, **Ham** and **Japheth**.*

Now our task here is to discover what these pressures were and when did we become so different. To answer this, we have to follow the tracks of Noah and his sons; and look for the change from wooly hair and dark skin to straight hair and light skin. The evolution of new languages, will also correlate to the new racial or cultural identities being forged.

---

[21] The journey of man: A genetic odyssey. Princeton, NJ: Princeton University Press, 2002. By Wells, Spencer PG 191

[22] The American Association of Physical Anthropologists meeting, held in Philadelphia, PA in March 2007 report by Ann Gibbons: European Skin Turned Pale Only Recently, Gene Suggests http://www.sciencemag.org/content/316/5823/364.1

[23] *Carlos Bustamante, a geneticist at Cornell University and his team,*

These are the families of the sons of Noah, after their generations, in their nations: and by these were the nations divided in the earth after the flood. Gen 10:32

Ham's sons returned to Africa after the flood and begun to build the empires of North East Africa. They are listed as the East and North-Eastern Africans. The Cushitic/*Kushites, Nubians* or sometimes grouped as Ethiopians, Egyptians or Mizraims, after the Arabic name for Egypt--Mizr, Punts or Punts identified as Somalians or Eritreans. Ham's youngest son Canaan fathered the Canaanites from the Levant region from Lebanon, Modern-day Israel, Saudi Arabia and Syria.

The descendants of Shem are traced through Abraham. They are traditionally identified as Semites or Jews. They remained among the East African descendants of Ham for many generations probably until the exodus from Egypt; and shared similar language and genetic markers until recently. This branch was previously referred to as the Hamito-Semitic branch with five language branches which are Berber, Cushitic, the extinct Egyptian-Coptic language, Chadic and Semitic (including Arabic and Hebrew).

[24]*The Lemba people of Africa carry, at a very high frequency, a particular genetic marker called the "Cohen modal haplotype," which is known to be characteristic of the paternally inherited Jewish priesthood.*

The Jewish descendants of Shem, form the final Semitic branch, and are marked off from the East of the Nile, to the Euphrates region, as they exit the garden out of slavery. The original negro/wooly haired sons from Adam to the African descendants of Ham, at the latter end of the story, become the lowest or basest of people. They later exit into slavery from the West.

The Semites also represent a literal Levitical priesthood, without an inheritance among the nations. They are charged with the responsibility to preserve the authenticity of the word. Thus extreme measures are taken to keep their populations small and deeply connected. As we continue to follow the trail of our divine guide, we discover the characteristics which mark the rise and fall of kingdoms. This corresponds with the entrance or exodus of the Jews and the evolution of theology.

Thus saith the Lord of hosts; In those days it shall come to pass, that ten men shall take hold out of all languages of the nations, even shall take hold of the skirt of him that is a Jew, saying, We will go with you: for we have heard that God is with you. Zechariah 8:4-23

In a few instances we will be deterred off of the trail to attend to the cries of agony from those left behind. There is a gradual decline or removal of the spirit as it transitions from one kingdom to the next; and a prophet or patriarch is always raised to proclaim this transition. These fallen Kingdoms begin with Abraham as he begins his journey out of Persia and the decline of ancient Kingdoms like Ur follow. Abraham then enters Egypt at the height of Egyptian civilization. Then he proceeds south into Nubia and Ethiopia (Genesis 13:1) and the story continues with Moses and the exodus of the Jews from Egypt, Daniel in Babylon, Zechariah and Ezra in Persia, Joel in Greece, Jesus from the Roman Empire, Phillip to the Ax mite Ethiopian Kingdom and Augustine into Europe.

The builders of a civilization are always immigrants and never the indigenous population.

---

[24] Y chromosomes traveling south: the cohen modal haplotype and the origins of the Lemba--the "Black Jews of Southern Africa". Thomas MG, Parfitt T, Weiss DA, Skorecki K, Wilson JF, le Roux M, Bradman N, Goldstein DB.
The Center for Genetic Anthropology, Departments of Biology and Anthropology, University College London, London, United Kingdom.

America represents the reunification of all the divided and scattered people of the world; and the new Tower which has been erected to commemorate the end of our journey.

These masons have built this tower without hands.

From this point on we have to rely entirely on the records left behind by the historians of the ages, because they provide the **only** historical records of these racial divisions. Their words, remains or drawings are the only information that anyone can use to draw an image of the ancient past. They tell us who people are and where they moved to, or colonized after they separated. Keep in mind that many nations were not always named as they are today.

The whole of Northern Europe, sometimes referred to as *North men,* were called Scythians until about the 2nd century. These were people, from Germany, Poland, Ukraine and Russia described as people with white skin, blue eyes and blonde hair. Then the French and English and tribes of North Western Europe were grouped together as Gauls, described as pale skinned people with red hair. Collectively these form one group which we will simply call European. The Southern regions, including all of Africa were originally populated by various features, shades and tribes from *the tanned copper like the San to the very dark*, with wooly or curly hair; but with distinct culture, tradition or character. The darkest people were called Ethiopians irrespective of their national origin.

The regions between the North and South are called the Mediterranean. This region includes Italy, Greece, Turkey and North Africa; and this is where the journey transitions into a game of checkers. Most of the people from the Mediterranean region are the ones providing the information about the people of the North and South; but the clues as to who they are and where they came from, require a bit more research. We will continue on the trail, by tracing the development of civilizations and study the migration of people. It is truly amazing how the demographics of every region has changed.

We start with Egypt because this was one of the first metropolis and certainly the most enduring civilization of all time. The greatest controversy of our time is the race of the ancient Egyptians. We know through their eyes what the people they came into contact with looked like, but what about themselves.

When we comb through the entire story of this civilization, their religion and culture as well as their images of themselves and the historians we first encounter, they **all** tell us that the ancient Egyptians were like most Africans. They were most certainly negros.

Egyptians then and now:

Figure 7 a) Old Kingdom Pharaoh Kufu, Khêops or Cheops 4th dynasty 2580 B.C. (Egyptian Museum), Berlin by Einsamer Schütze b). Woman from the Lower Valley of the Omo River, Southern Ethiopia. UNESCO World Heritage Site, Source Vittorio Bianchi by AnnaMaria Donnoli c).Pharaohic hair dress. Egyptian Museum), Berlin by Einsamer Schütze d). Maasai man from Ethiopia.

The Egyptians 3000-500 BC

Figure 8 a). Isis Nursing Horus, Brooklyn Museum, Charles Edwin Wilbour Fund, 37.400E: b).Sun God Ra and Amun by Dennis Jarvis: c). Fresco of Tuthmosis III 1504 B.C. morphed with the Fertility God Min By Cris.real293: d).11th dynasty army tomb of Mesehti, Cairo Egyptian Museum by Udimu

When Egypt, Cush, their brothers and families immigrated back to East Africa, they were surprised to find a remnant of the ancient elders there. Their story of survival was a remarkable one. When their homes begun to flood, God heard their cries and sent a great serpent. The serpent carried them to the top of a mountain and there they saw giant men as tall as trees. This is the place they called the mountain of the Gods. When they got there, the waters came suddenly and stopped about half way to the top. Then a great earthquake broke off a huge chunk of land in Europe and a tsunami pushed the already submerged region further under water, everyone and every animal died.

After the water withdrew, Min took them out of the ground and breathed life back into them and they watched him do the same to some of the animals. For this reason they worshiped Min as their savior, the God of regeneration. From around 4000 BC the guidance of the serpent and the grace of Min were celebrated throughout the land. [25] *The emblem of Min, appears, prior to his anthropomorphic iconography, on predynastic monuments such as standards on boats painted on Naqada II pottery.*

[26]*At first, (as some of the priests have fabulously reported), the Gods and demi-Gods reigned in Egypt for the space of eighteen thousand years, the last of which was Orus the son of Isis. Afterwards, they say that men reigned there for the space of fifteen thousand years. Thus the first kings were considered literal Gods, and their descendants, sons of God who continued in their image.* Though Min was worshiped throughout dynastic history, other Gods emerged to supplement the various roles of their spiritual world as they perceived it. *Among the variation were Ptah, creator of all things, Ra the Sun God, and Amun or Amon was one of the most popular, he was the self-created God.*

[27]*There are some paintings which occur chiefly in Upper Egypt where the black and red faces hold a singular relation to each other. This singular representation is often repeated in all the Egyptian temples, but only here at Philae and at Elephantine with this*

---

[25] The Routledge Dictionary of Egyptian Gods and Goddesses. Associate Professor of English George Hart, George Hart Routledge, Mar 31, 2005 pg. 93

[26] The Historical Library of Diodorus the Sicilian: In Fifteen Books. To which are Added the Fragments of Diodorus, and Those Published by H. Valesius, I. Rhodomannus, & F. Ursinus, translated by G Booth ESQ Harvard College Library In two volumes. Vol. 1 printed by W.M Dowall 1814 by Diodorus (Siculus.) page 29 -50

[27] Researches Into the Physical History of Mankind: In Two Volumes, Volume 1 by James Cowles Prichard 1826 pg.321

distinction of color, may commemorate the transmission of religious rites and social institutions from the Ethiopians to the Egyptians. There are three priests, two have black faces and hands and are pouring from two jars strings of alternate scepters of Osiris over the head of another whose face is red. But in both cases one is invariably older than the other, and appears to be of superior divinity. Mr. Hamilton conjectures that such figures represent the communication of religious rites from Ethiopia to Egypt. The black figures are most frequently conferring the symbols of divinity and sovereignty on the latter.

For now we will assume that the ancient portrait looked as varied as the images below, but there are more clues which will help to determine the accuracy of our assumptions.

Ethnographic Portrait of ancient Africa

1.Fulani/Wodaabe women, in Niger. by Dan Lundberg
2.Touareg woman in Akoubounou, Niger. by Rebecca Gustafson. Pliny says they are the descendants of Hercules.
3. Zulu girl in South Africa by Svdmolen
4. South Ndebele women from the Mapumalanga higveld (Botshibelo). By Hein waschefort
5.woman in Namibia. by Nicolas M. Perrault (San) Pliny considers the San peope *Leucaethiopes* because of the light skin.
6. sangoma women in Zululand by Wizzy
7.Fula, Fulani, Fulbe, Peul, or Fulaw women in Paoua, by Brice Blondel, HDPTCAR
8. Himba woman, Mbapaa, by Jescapism
Himbas paint themselves red with a otjize, a mixture of butter and ochre, as a sun block.
9.South African Rain Queen Makobo Constance Modjadji VI MichaelStreaton Photography

Some Africans paint themselves red with a product which the ancients called vermillion, like the Himba. These people say that they are of [28]*Trojan extraction*. Others paint themselves Gold and red, like the

---

[28] Earth and Its Inhabitants, West Africa Elisée Reclus, Ernest George Ravenstein, Augustus Henry Keane D. Appleton, 1892 pg. 358

Fulani. Egyptians also depicted themselves in red and gold like the Fulani and Himba people, as well as the darkest black associated with Ethiopians. Some were said to be without noses like the San (in image 5) others without necks like the Ndebele (in image 4).

[29] The term Kanuri, current in the country for centuries, designates not a particular race, but simply the more civilized residents, in whom have been gradually merged the various ethnical elements. The sense of the word is unknown although popular etymology referred to the Arabic nur, light, whence Ka-nurior people of the light earned their mission of illuminators amid the darkness of the surrounding heathen world.

Figure 9 Wodaabe cross dressing men (Madea's of Africa). Ancient Ritual performed to attract a female mate by Bappah

Africans are virtually erased from many courses of study today; but that was not the case in the beginning of historical record keeping. [30]The Ethiopians received high acalades by almost all historians. Lucian, considered them *wiser than all others, experts in astrology, with a knowledge of the heavens that they transmitted to the Egyptians.*

Romance writters like Pseudo-Callisthenes and Helidorus, cast the Ethiopians in a utopia. Greeks regarded them as antiquity, Herodotus and Diodorus reported that, all the gods traveled to Ethiopia to receive a solem feast prepared for them by the Ethiopians. The modern strategy lumps all Africans together, as primitive and undeveloped, while severing Egyptians from Nubians and Nubians from Ethiopians. This division masterfully obscures the African identity.

[31] All the regions south of Dongola are embraced under the name of Soudan-an immense region stretching across the entire continent of Africa, on both sides of the equator, and subdivided by geographers into Eastern, Central and western Soudan. The name is derived from the Arabic Aswad, black, of which the plural is suda; so that Beled-es-Soudan means simply country of the blacks.

[29] Earth and Its Inhabitants, West Africa Elisée Reclus, Ernest George Ravenstein, Augustus Henry Keane D. Appleton, 1892 pg. 358
[30] Rethinking the Other in Antiquity Erich S. Gruen Princeton University Press, Aug 27, 2012
[31] Journal of the American Geographical Society of New York, Volume 17 The Society, 1885 pg. 131-134

In dynastic Egypt there are more than two and a half millennia of history, but only about one hundred and seventy Pharaohs. This is the clearest evidence of their lifespan. Abraham is said to have lived for one hundred and seventy five years and one Pharaoh Pepi, reigned for about a hundred years, while a great number reigned for decades. This makes it very easy to align Egyptian history to the biblical narrative. The accounts from Abraham through Moses were passed down for generations by the Jews in Egypt. Then this expanse of time is divided into dynasties, which represent a particular blood line from each founder.

Each pharaoh claimed his decent from one of the Gods and became the living image of him. Their names were also a derivative of the persona of God they embodied. Through this divine channel, they developed an advanced understanding of the world; and recorded a prevalent and perceptible, force which guided and instructed them to achieve great success.

Figure 10 Pharaoh Djoser Image by Jon Bodworth

Pharaoh Djoser/Dozer (left) was the first Pharaoh of the 3rd dynasty. Advancements to astronomy including the creation of the calendar very similar to what we use today, have been credited to his reign. He ruled for 28 years from 2661 B.C. and commissioned one of his top officials as the architect to oversee the construction of the step pyramid. The pyramid design seems to be the ancient obsession with finding the mountain of the Gods as described by the elders. [32]According to some, *the Step Pyramid was a ladder not a symbol of a ladder but an actual one.*

The bible records that Jacob the grandson of Abraham dreamed, *and behold a ladder set up on the earth, and the top of it reached to heaven: and behold the angels of God ascending and descending on it.* Gen 28:12 This area in Bethel of Israel is considered the *gate* into Heaven or Eden. Jacob also wrestled with one of these beings. Djoser's chief architect, vizier and doctor, Imhotep has been one of the candidates for the role of Joseph son of Jacob; but the dates would not align if this ladder was the pyramid described by his father, Jacob. This pyramid is also contemporary with Babel and Mohenjo-Daro which would have been a few generations before Abraham.

---

[32] Mysteries of History by Robert Stewart PHD with Clint Twist and Edward Horton. National Geographic Project

Most scholars (including the editors of the King James Bible published by Zondervan and Dr. Ian Barnes author of "The Historical Atlas of the Bible", believe that Abraham lived around 2000B.C. This aligns within the reign of Mentuhotep a Pharaoh of the 11th dynasty. Mentuhotep II reigned for 51 years 2046 BC – 1995BC, and he claimed his descent from Min. His reign is marked by the beginning of a unified and prosperous Egypt; thus this is most probably the Pharaoh of Abraham. His divinity and power were still petitioned years after his death by Pharaohs Senusret/ Sesostris III who ruled for forty years from 1878 BC to 1839 B.C. and Amenemhat III who ruled for forty five years from 1842 to 1797 B.C. both observed the symbolic opening of the mouth ceremony on his statue.

The painting of Abraham, below is from a book containing reproductions of a fresco painted in an ancient palace in Mari, Syria. [33]*Dating from the early second millennium B.C. which is believed to be the right period for Abraham, the palace—along with tens of thousands of cuneiform tablets—was excavated in 1933.*

Figure 11 a). Mentuhotep II (Morphed with Marcus Carvey) at Metropolitan Museum of Art /image by Keith Schengili-Roberts: b).Earliest depiction of Abraham from the world's oldest preserved Jewish synagogue in Dura-Europos dated by an Aramaic inscription to 244. Fresco of Abraham from the 3rd-century synagogue, now at the National Museum of Damascus: c).Bust of Senusret III at the Munich Museum by Einsamer Schutze: d). Amenemhat III image by George Shuklin

Mentuhotep II provides the bible's first mention of domesticated cattle; [34]which is believed to have begun in the Nabta Playa region. When Abraham entered Egypt with his wife, Mentuhotep II wanted to have her as his own (Genesis 12:14 -15);

And he entreated Abram well for her sake: and he had sheep, and oxen, and he asses, and menservants, and maidservants, and she asses, and camels; (Genesis 12:16) but he contracted an illness which the bible calls a plague. This plague may have come with Abraham from the Assyrian region.

In Genesis 6:2 we learnt that the entertainment of foreigners was prophesied to eventually become the demise of the Pharaohs. Thus the pharaohs were admonished to select a queen among their darker people. This eventually led to the custom, that Pharaoh would select a Nubian Queen as a means of solidifying their two nations. The chief queen among their many wives was called God's wife; and only

---

[33] http://ngm.nationalgeographic.com/features/world/asia/israel/abraham-text.html report By Tad Szulc

[34] Johnson AL. 2002. Cross-Cultural Analysis of Pastoral Adaptations and Organizational States.
Wendorf F, and Schild R. 1998. Nabta Playa and Its Role in Northeastern African Prehistory.
Stock F, and Gifford-Gonzalez D. 2013. Genetics and African Cattle Domestication. See complete credits in end notes.

God's wife could bare the son of God and wield the mighty serpent. This is also the origin of the biblical title *Queen of the South.* Luke 11:31

In many African nations, a man secures a bride from her father, in exchange for a great quantity of cattle.

[35]And for her (Isis') sake it is a custom among them, that they honor a queen and allow her more power and authority than a king: in their contracts of marriage authority is given to the wife over her husband, at which time the husbands promise to be obedient to their wives in all things.

Figure 12 (L)Empress Zewditu I was the "Queen of Kings" and daughter of Menelek II who was the last monarch in direct agnatic descent from the Solomonic dynasty from 1916 and 1930.Her successor Haile Selassie was also linked to the Solomonic dynasty by the maternal line to Queen of Sheba.
(R) Portrait of Ras Makonnen Woldemikael and his son Lij Tafari Makonnen/Haile Selassie I Emperor of Ethiopia from 1930 to 1974. ByHarold G. Marcus Haile Selassie I: the formative years, 1892-1936. — Red Sea Press, 1995

Abraham's first son Ishmael was born of an Egyptian mother. Solomon and Mohamed the patriarch of Islam also married Egyptian women. In *The Songs of Solomon,* Solomon writes love letters to his Queen who complains of scorn from the fairer daughters of Jerusalem. The last heir to his union with the Queen of Sheba, is believed to have been Halle Selassie king of Ethiopia.

Ethiopians believe that the Ark of the Covenant was brought from Jerusalem by the son of the Queen of [36]Sheba. Many people in the African diaspora have maintained oral traditions that they are the exiled children of [37]Zion.

Are ye not as children of the Ethiopians to me, O children of Israel? Amos 9:7.

This unified identity, is maintained through equal mentions of Ethiopia and Ethiopians as it is with Israel and the Israelites in the bible.

The Igbo of Nigeria in West Africa, believe that their name means "Hebrew" [38]*and the Jews of each Nation have different ways of pronouncing Hebrew.*

The Lemba people mentioned earlier, are South Eastern Africans, with a genetic connection to the priesthood of Moses; and [39] the Ethiopian Orthodox Church, claims a religion rooted in the Old Testament with 1,000 years of Judaism, followed by 2,000 years of Christianity.

---

[35] The Historical Library of Diodorus the Sicilian: In Fifteen Books. To which are Added the Fragments of Diodorus, and Those Published by H. Valesius, I. Rhodomannus, & F. Ursinus, translated by G Booth ESQ Harvard College Library In two volumes. Vol. 1 printed by W.M Dowall 1814 by Diodorus (Siculus.) chpt 11 pg 33.]

[36] Marcus Haile Sellassie I: the formative years, 1892-1936. By Harold G.— Red Sea Press, 1995 Royal Genealogies, Or the Genealogical Tables of Emperors, Kings and Princes by James Anderson Bettenham, 1732

[37] The children of Zion may be a tribe which Diodorus identified as the Southern Ethiopians, who are *"all have sound bodies because they kill off the lame and old among them."* A cultural correlation to King David, who must also display this antagonism towards the lame, to acquire one of the strongholds "Mount Zion" from the Jebusites. 2Samuel 5:4-8 The Jebusites were probably the Ethiopians of Gerar, who pursued king Asa in 2Chronicles 14

[38] A new voyage to Italy: with curious observations on several other countries, as: Germany, Switzerland, Savoy, Geneva, Flanders, and Holland; together with useful instructions for those who shall travel thither, Volume 1, Part 1 Maximilien Misson Printed for R. Bonwicke, 1714 pg140

[39] Raffaele, Paul (December 2007). "Keepers of the Lost Ark? " http://www.smithsonianmag.com/people-places/ark-covenant-200712.html#ixzz2WLmkS9jD

After Abraham left Egypt *Genesis 13:1* says he journeyed *South* with the wealth of cattle silver and gold which he acquired in Egypt. This is perhaps the region of Sudan which correlates to the development of Kush or prehistoric Nubia. Just about a century ago a geographer said that:

The so-called island of Meroe was formerly the center of a civilization older than the pharaohs. Standing upon the site of the ancient city, I counted no less than forty-two pyramids-smaller, it is true, than those of Gizah, but of a size to be considered gigantic in any other land.

If Abraham fathered Isaac at a hundred then Joseph, Abraham's grandson may have arrived in Egypt during the reign of Senusret III who ruled from 1878 BC to 1839 B.C.

[40]Many scholars place Joseph in the 12th dynasty under Sesostris III. Joseph may have been brought in as a slave towards the end of his reign.

[41]*And he employed none of the Egyptians in his works, but finished all by the labors of the captives; and therefore he caused an inscription to be made upon all the temples thus-"None of the natives were put to labor here."*

This underscores the irony of the jest that slavery begun in Africa. It also illustrates that slavery was not initially based on race, and was not as inhumane as it became later. These slaves were like minimum wage earners, able to work their way out of slavery. This is what happened to Joseph, he was originally sold into slavery, but raised in rank to be second to Pharaoh. *And Pharaoh said unto his servants, Can we find such a one as this is, a man in whom the Spirit of God is?* Genesis 41:38

Other evidence of Joseph's timeline is the canal which was built:

[42]*whose ruins to this day bear the name Bahr Yusef ("River of Joseph").* [43]Merrill believes that *the very name survives as a testimony to the contribution of Joseph to the public-works projects of Sesostris.*

Senusret III was also one of the most ambitious and prosperous Pharaohs in Egypt.

Senusret III named Sesostris by Diodorus; *was the first Egyptian that built long ships. By the help of this fleet, he gained all the islands in this sea, and subdued the bordering nations as far as to India. Then he subdued the Scythians as far as to the river Tanais, which divides Europe from Asia; where they say he left some of his Egyptians at the lake Moetis, and gave origin to the nations of Colchis; and to prove that they were originally Egyptians, they bring this argument, that they are circumcised after the manner of the Egyptians, which custom continued in this colony as it did among the Jews. Thence passing over into Europe, he was in danger of losing his whole army, through the difficulty of the passages, and want of provisions. And, therefore, putting a stop to his expedition in Thrace, up and down in all his conquests, he erected pillars, where on were inscribed, in Egyptian letters,*

[40] Kingdom of Priests: A History of Old Testament Israel Eugene H. Merrill, Baker Academic, Mar 1, 2008 pg66
[41] The Historical Library of Diodorus the Sicilian: In Fifteen Books. To which are Added the Fragments of Diodorus, and Those Published by H. Valesius, I. Rhodomannus, & F. Ursinus, translated by G Booth ESQ Harvard College Library In two volumes. Vol. 1
[42] The Cambridge Ancient History: Early history of the Middle East. Volume 1. Part 2, Volume 1
I. E. S. Edwards, Cyril John Gadd, Nicholas Geoffrey Lemprière Hammond Cambridge University Press, 1971 pg 510
[43] Kingdom of Priests: A History of Old Testament Israel Eugene H. Merrill, Baker Academic, Mar 1, 2008 pg67#91

called hieroglyphics, these words:-"Sesostris, king of kings, and lord of lords, subdued the "country by his arms.'

A bust of a nobleman from this dynasty was discovered by an Egyptologist coincidentally named Jack A. *Josephson.*

Figure 13 Hyksos entering Egypt depicted on top, and Egyptians below.
By Kurohito (Own work) [GFDL (http://www.gnu.org/copyleft/fdl.html) or CC- 2.0

A tomb which contains the images of people called the Hyksos entering Egypt, is believed to commemorate the arrival of Joseph's father and his family. There is little difference between the Hyksos (illustrated above) and the Egyptians (below), besides their attire: the Jewish tunic of many colors (Gen37:3).

From then on the Hyksos settled in Egypt as the family of Joseph did. They eventually rose to power leading Joseph to proclaim that God sent him to Egypt to become *father to Pharaoh*s, *lord of his entire household and ruler of all Egypt.* Gen 45:8

[44]*Horses enabled the Hyksos, to conquer then horseless Egypt, and to establish themselves temporarily as pharaohs.*

Manetho, 3rd century BC was an Egyptian historian and priest who tells us that [45]*Hyksos* means *Sheppard kings*, and they reigned in Egypt for five hundred and eleven years and were finally shut up in a place called Avaris until they were forced out. The Egyptians say that the Jews were forced out, but the bible tells us they left; both versions confirm an exodus.

---

[44] Guns, Germs, and Steel: The Fates of Human Societies by Jared Diamond 1999 pg. 91
[45] The Complete Works of Flavius-Josephus the Celebrated Jewish Historian by William Whiston 1895 (Against Apion book 1)

The Hyksos ruled for about a century and were finally expelled by the founder of the New Kingdom 18th dynasty Pharaoh Ahmose I (a king who did not to Know Joseph).

[46]*His triumphant return however, was greeted with the news of outbreaks among the remains of the Hyksos people. The expulsion of a race as a whole cannot be effected after several centuries of occupation; and though the foreign armies might be driven out, there must have been a large part of the population of mixed race, ready to tolerate the Egyptians if they were conquerors, but preferring an independent life.*
The remaining Hyksos left in Egypt were then enslaved.

The Woman and the Serpent

The veneration of Aahmes, and still more for his sister and wife Nefertari, was long continued, and is still more frequent than that for any other ruler. It is seen that Nefertari was adored as a divinity on the same footing as the great Gods of Thebes. She had a priesthood, and a large sacred shrine on a bark borne in processions;
[47]*A measure of her importance was her posthumous veneration at Thebes, where later pharaohs were depicted offering to her as a goddess among the gods.*

After the death of Ahmose I (Aahmes I), Nefertari governed jointly with her son Amenhotep I, the second King of Egypt's 18th Dynasty.

[48]During the New Kingdom the dialect undergoes some changes, probably due to the century of Hyksos rule. This transition in the dialect is referred to as Late Egyptian, *and it differs considerably from Mid Egyptian owing to the incorporation of many new features from the spoken language of the period.*

Figure 14 Honored God's Wife of Ammon Ahmose-Nofretari full sister of Ahmose, holdin the staff of the serpent.

The natives may have tried to counteract this changing identity, so that Nefertari, is depicted in the blackest of tints, which celebrated Egyptian superiority and omniscience. The term KMT *"Black Land,"* also begins to appear with great frequency [49]*as the term for the entire country as well as for its personification.* This spelled extreme prejudice against non-Egyptians, especially *Asiatics*; and the beginning of racism. This type of idolatry, may have been an outrage to a jealous creator, who would later stipulate a command against it.

---

[46] A History of Egypt: During the XVIIth and XVIIIth Dynasties. 1896, with Additions to 1898, Sir William Matthew Flinders Petrie, Charles Schribner's Sons, 1897 pg. 35-38
[47] http://www.britannica.com/EBchecked/topic/180468/ancient-Egypt/22306/The-13th-dynasty-c-1756-c-1630-bc
[48] The Cambridge Ancient History, by Iorwerth Eiddon Stephen Edwards, I. E. S. Edwards, C. J. Gadd, N. G. L. Hammond. Cambridge University Press, Dec 2, 1970 pg133
[49] Ancient Near Eastern, Biblical, and Judaic Studies in Honor of Baruch A. Levine
Baruch A. Levine, Robert Chazan, William W. Hallo, Lawrence H. Schiffman Eisenbrauns, Jan 1, 1999 pg. 40

Egyptians begun to represent the differences which were becoming more apparent among people of different nations at this time. [50]Libyans were depicted as light skinned negroes, somewhat like anti-colonialist, President Muammar al-Gaddafi.

Libya is not named as a son of Ham, so we may assume that the lighter Libyans diffused out of Egypt. The *Dark skin*, which is now characteristic of Africans, was evidently acquired through their aggressive selection preferences.

Most Africans were distinguished by their customs, but the darkest people were all grouped together as Ethiopian (*dark skinned people*). Herodotus classified two groups of Ethiopians.

Figure 15 (L) Libyan man from the palace of Tell el-Yahoudiyeh, in the Nile delta, reign of Rameses III (1184–1153 BC, 20th Dynasty) 3200 years ago. (R) Deceased President Gaddafi

[51]*Eastern Etiopians were different from the Southern Ethiopians and likewise from the Asiatic Ethiopians, or those of the Colchis; for their hair was straight.*

Figure 16 a).Western Ethiopian Maasai woman carrying her baby in traditional clothing and jewelry in the Serengeti National Park, Tanzania by Petronas, William Warby from London, England b). Eastern Ethiopian woman and child in Madagascar by Steve Evans

From the Egyptians to Pliny 100 AD up until the 19th century the ethnographic portrait of Africa changes very little. Although the names of the tribes differ, many of the characteristics and customs remained and do not seem to have been greatly altered. The general consensus was that the African continent was populated mostly by *"Ethiopians"* who were seperated only by the Sahara desert.

Within the context of a global separation of races, Egyptians boasted in their black skins. This was the color of the soil from which man was created. This was the great land of black people (*remetch en Kermet),* Nubia or Bilad-al-Sudan means *country of the blacks in Arabic* and Ethiopia or Aethiopia means *sun burnt* in Greek.

---

[50] Libyan man from the palace of Tell el-Yahoudiyeh, in the Nile delta, reign of Rameses III (1184–1153 BC, 20th Dynasty) 3200 years ago. Now in Louvre Museum, Department of Egyptian antiquities, Sully, by Guillaume Blanchard
[51] The Nine Books of the History of Herodotus, Volume 2 by Henry Slatter, 1837 pg. 376

Figure 17 a). Eighteenth dynasty Amenhotep III in British Museum, London by Benkid77. b).God's Wife Tiye in a wooly afro (Egyptian Museum) Berlin by Einsamer Schütze. c). Their son Akhenaten (Morphed with US President Obama) Image taken at the Altes Museum, Berlin. By Keith Schengili-Roberts

This kingdom represents nearly 500 years of political stability and economic prosperity, and an abundance of artistic masterpieces. In 1386 BC, Amenhotep III began his reign and continued for thirty four years with unprecedented peace and prosperity. God's wife Tiye, was married to Amenhotep at a very young age; but was deserted when Amenhotep ignored the ancient prophecy. Amen married foreign women, from Syria, Babylon and Mitanni. One of his scarabs records that one of his many foreign concubines, arrived in Egypt accompanied by more than three hundred women.

From then on, the Negro women of Egypt began to hide their afros in shame by covering their heads with wigs and hair weaves made from the hair of the more desirable women.

[52] *Quantities of human hair dating from the Presynaptic to the Roman period have frequently been found within a funerary context despite their frequent omission from exaction reports. There is little evidence for the use of false hair from the old kingdom but by the New Kingdom, braids and wigs become precious commodities listed alongside incense and gold in the 'accounts list' from the town of Kahun.*

Tiye's mummy was discovered with one of these wigs. Wigs or extensions remain a hallmark of women, particularly African women in diverse cultures. These new women undoubtedly contributed to a change in the ancient culture, language and traditions of the Egyptians.

Towards the end of the 18th dynasty, the Egyptians also felt threatened by the growing population of monotheistic Israelites. The Pharaohs had grown proud and lazy from years of slave labor as well as divine providence; and could feel the spirits' power slipping from their land.

Come, we must deal shrewdly with them or they will become even more numerous and, if war breaks out, will join our enemies, fight against us and leave the country. Exodus 1:10
The bible says that the Egyptians resorted to genocide to keep the population of Israelites under control.

By the 14th century BC foreign Gods like Qadesh and Baal, made their way into Egyptian theology. Pharaoh Amenhotep IV (1352-1336 B.C) abolished the entire priesthood and adopted the first monotheistic theology. This placed him at odds with the old establishment. Amen also changed his name to Akhenaten, the spirit of Aten the only God. Akhenaten's expulsion of the ancient priesthood also coincides with the appearance of the Olmecs, in Central/Meso America along similar lines of latitude as Egypt and Kush.

---

[52] Ancient Egyptian Materials and Technology edited by Paul T. Nicholson, Ian Shaw chapter 20 page 495. Hair Joann Fletcher. (Griffith 1898:39,48-50. Pls, xix-xx)

Figure 18 a). Olmec Head in the Jalapa anthropological museum of Xalapa by Frank C. Müller, Baden-Baden: b).A young chieftain Veracruz culture.ca. 300 - 600 AD Art Institute of Chicago by Madman2001: c).The Pyramid of The Sun and Avenue of The Dead, an ancient civilization Teotihuacán, Mexico D.F by Selefant d). Bonampak Temple in Mexico

[53]The Olmecs are believed to be one of the first Meso Americans, like the Egyptians they share a love for the colossal images of themselves. This later became the home of the Incas and Aztecs. They also celebrated a serpent, bird named Quetzalcoatl, who sits at the base of their step pyramid.

José Melgar, discovered the first colossal head in 1862 and attributed this head to a "Negro race". [54]Ivan van Sertima discovered a pre-Columbian, African presence in the Americas and Dr. Clarence Weiant assistant archeologist in on the National Geographic-Smithsonian expedition to Tres Zapotes agreed.

[55]The first Europeans to arrive in North America give us this description of Native Americans in Maryland:

They are of dark color not much unlike the Ethiopians, and hair black and thick, and not very long, which they tie together back on the head in the shape of a little tail. As for symmetry of the men, they are well proportioned, of medium stature, and rather exceed us. They are broad, arms well built, the legs and other parts of the body well put together...they incline to broadness of the face... but not all, for in more we saw the face clear cut. The eyes black and large, the glance intent and quick. And the greatest Runners.
From what we are able to learn they resemble in the last two respects the Orientals of the farthest Sinarian regions.

Figure 19 Pyramids in South America and Egypt

In St.Lucian mythology, the high priest, had a map of the world. Standing in Africa, he then jumped over a large basin filled with water, which represents the ocean and the exterior of the basin represented land. If he fell into the basin he would drown, but if he ended up on the other side of the basin he would reach the other side of the ocean. With no return ticket home, many of us were already here.

---

[53]America's First Civilization Ancient peoples and places / ISSN 1462-4869 by Richard A. Diehl

[54] They Came Before Columbus African Studies professor Ivan van Sertima of Rutgers University/Dr. Clarence Weiant (1897-1986) published his findings in May 1977 in the New York Times

[55] The New Larned History for Ready Reference, Reading and Research: The Actual Words of the World's Best Historians, Volume 1 Josephus Nelson Larned 1524- Page 273 Verranzano's voyage along the Atlantic coast of North America. This Italian navigator was the first *European* to sight New York and Narragansett bays.

(The Chinese are believed to have made it to the New World, as early as the 11th century.

*In the various editions of the Norvus Orbis, which detail Amerigo Vespucci's four voyages, Ramusio has given an abridgement in Italian of the third and fourth voyages only (his attention being chiefly directed to the results of Southern and African explorations).

*The First Four Voyages of Amerigo Vespucci By Amerigo Vespucci

After the death of Akhenaton, the Armana religion came to an end and the people once again returned to their old traditions. Their rejection of the next phase of maturity, is the beginning of the spirits transition from Egypt. This is also the beginning of the first monotheistic Doctrine in Persia-Zoroastrianism.

*During that long period, (*the 19th dynasty', 67 year reign of Ra-moses II from 1279 – 1213) *the king of Egypt died. The Israelites groaned in their slavery and cried out, and their cry for help because of their slavery went up to God.* Exodus 2:23

Ramses II had one of the most prosperous, hence the most labor intensive governments.

Figure 20 Earliest depiction of Moses and the Jews crossing the Red Sea. Dura EuRopas

The exodus of the Jews probably begun at the end of his reign 1213 BC. God implanted Moses among the Egyptians to remove the Jews from Egypt. While Moses hated the way the Egyptians were treating the Jews, he probably had no idea that he too, was a Jew. He was raised and educated by the Egyptians and was able to pass in every way as a natural Egyptian. We can only imagine the isolation he felt, being rejected by the Jews and seen as a traitor to the Egyptians.

God instructed Moses: *And thou shalt say unto Pharaoh, Thus saith the Lord, Israel is my son, even my firstborn: And I say unto thee, Let my son go, that he may serve me: and if thou refuse to let him go, behold, I will slay thy son, even thy firstborn.* Exodus 4:22-23

But the Egyptians would not relinquish their power peacefully, Moses had to produce the serpent as a sign. *So Moses and Aaron went to Pharaoh and did just as the Lord commanded. Aaron threw his staff down in front of Pharaoh and his officials, and it became a snake. Pharaoh then summoned wise men and sorcerers, and the Egyptian magicians also did the same things by* their secret arts*: Each one threw down his staff and it became a snake. But Aaron's staff swallowed up their staffs.* Ex 7:10

Moses thus illustrates the wisdom and power of his serpent, which has surpassed that of the Egyptians. He also marries an [56]*Ethiopian* woman, whose offspring would then replace the priesthood of the Egyptians. *His sons were named of the tribe of Levi* (1 Chronicles 23:14) *and at that time the Lord* separated *the tribe of Levi, to bear the ark of the covenant of the Lord, to stand before the Lord to minister unto him, and to bless in his name, unto this day.* Deuteronomy 10:8 Moses' father in law also served as a minister unto him, this illustrates that the Midianites were a spiritually powerful people.

---

[56] (Numbers 12) Ethiopian here may refer to race and not nationality, because Moses' wife was from Medea/Midia was a city of the colchis. The Medes later gave birth to the Persian Empire.

The Egyptians continued to pursue the fleeing Jews, but the passage which admitted the Jews through the Red Sea closed in and killed many of them.

And the Lord went before them by day in a pillar of a cloud, to show them the way; and by night in a pillar of fire, to give them light; to go by day and night: Exodus 13:2

The Jews encountered Plagues in the course of their journey, which killed many thousands of their people Numbers 16 and 25

So *the children of Israel took all the women of Midian captives, and their little ones, and took the spoil of all their cattle, and all their flocks, and all their goods. Numbers 31:9*

Judaism was grafted out of Egypt, as the accredited theology; and the laws of their distinguished nation were engraved on stone by the hand of God. At the exodus of Jews from Egypt, one of the most important commands that God lays down is their absolute segregation. This was done to trace the identity of the Jews, as a distinct people and to preserve the authenticity of the word until this day.

Take heed to thyself, lest thou make a covenant with the inhabitants of the land whither thou goest, lest it be for a snare in the midst of thee: But ye shall destroy their altars, break their images, and cut down their groves: For thou shalt worship no other god: for the LORD, whose name is Jealous, is a jealous God: Exodus 34: 12-16

But when: the children of Israel dwelt among the Canaanites, Hittites, and Amorites, and Perizzites, and Hivites, and Jebusites: they took their daughters to be their wives, and gave their daughters to their sons, and served their gods. Judges 3: 5-6

This means that the entire Middle Eastern region are one people, who share the same history and background from Moses and the prophets. *For they have taken of their daughters for themselves, and for their sons: so that the holy seed have mingled themselves with the people of those lands*: Ezra 9:2

Since the age of King David, a decree was issued against the people of the Middle East.

Now therefore the sword shall never depart from thine house. 2 Samuel 12:10

There will Never be peace in this region. (This is because) The Lord hath mingled a perverse spirit in the midst thereof: Isaiah 19:14

Figure 21 a) Egyptian representation of a Habiru or a Hebrew b) Yasser Arafat Palestinian leader by Hans Jørn Storgaard Andersen

[57]This word became the compass which guided our civilizations development of laws, ethics, morality and democracy; it set off every revolution in history since the exodus and gave birth to three of the worlds' religions: Judaism, Christianity and Islam. It also contains laws against many of the practices of the Africans.

[58]*Its significance on Western culture, language and thought is incalculable.*
The greatest archaeological breakthrough in discovering texts was undoubtedly the discovery of the Dead Sea scrolls in 1947. The scrolls were found in a cave near the Dead Sea and finally identified as Hebrew texts. One of them was a copy of the book of Isaiah. When compared to the Masoretic texts, various differences were found but on the whole there were no major changes and the discovery tended to give greater authority to the accuracy of the Jewish copyists.

The Book of Isaiah, is also one of the most comprehensive and prophetical writings of the Old Testament. With messages which span several generations from the announcement of Tirhakah as king to the birth of Christ and beyond. This extensive coverage of time has led scholars to believe that there were other prophets who continued in the calling of Isaiah after his death.

According to 6:1, Isaiah received his call "in the year that King Uzziah died" (742 BC), and his latest recorded activity is dated in 701 BC. Only chapters 1-39, however, can be assigned to this period. Chapters 40-66 are much later in origin and therefore known as Deutero-Isaiah (Second Isaiah). Encyclopedia Britannica

Figure 22 Middle East

---

[57]Let us with caution indulge the supposition that morality can be maintained without religion. Reason and experience both forbid us to expect that national morality can prevail in exclusion of religious principle.
George Washington First President of the United States.
[58]The Historical Atlas of the Bible by Dr. Ian Barnes

After the exodus from Egypt the Spirit began to seek out a new home and dispatched Jonah to Assyria.

The Assyrians were well known for brutality and barbarianism, and so this request was resisted by the prophet.

The lord replied in Jonah 4:11

And should not I spare Nineveh, that great city, wherein are more than six score thousand persons that cannot discern between their right hand and their left hand; and also much cattle?

Figure 23 Graven image of Dagon as a merman, from a Bas relief at the Louvre

The Assyrians idolized the fish as a God; so when Jonah entered into Nineveh the capital city of the Assyrians, the story of his emerging from the bosom of a great fish preceded him; and his warning of the destruction ordained for the empire was heeded, because, it came from God, as they understood him.

At this time a cry came from Nubia, it was the voice of Taharqa; the spirit of God turned back to Egypt.

Isaiah (740-698 BC) Isaiah foretold of Taharqa as king, when he was still the general of the Egyptian army, around 700 B.C. He didn't become Pharaoh until 690 B.C. to 664 B.C. (2 Kings 19:9; Isaiah 37:9)

Taharqa's cries averted the induction of the Assyrians and turned the face of God back towards Egypt and the Ethiopians.

Therefore thus saith the Lord God of hosts, O my people that dwellest in Zion, be not afraid of the Assyrian: he shall smite thee with a rod, and shall lift up his staff against thee, after the manner of Egypt. For yet a very little while, and the indignation shall cease, and mine anger in their destruction.

Isaiah 10:23-25

Taharqa's humility and complete reliance on God could not be ignored, and he was rewarded with a remarkable reign.

Dr. Ivan Van Sertima said that:

[59]*It is this same Taharka referred to in early Spanish chronicles as Tarraco that led a garrison into Spain and invaded it during this period.*

By most historical accounts he was one of the greatest military tacticians of the ancient world.

[60] *Ethiopians sent great forces abroad into other countries where they succeeded in bringing many parts of the world under their dominion....*

---

[59] The Golden Age of the Moor by Ivan Van Sertima /Transaction Publishers, 1992 page 2
[60] Race and the Writing of History: Riddling the Sphinx: Maghan Keita Assistant Professor of History and Director of Africana Studies Villanova University Social Science -Oxford University Press, Nov 6, 2000

Figure 24 Wall paintings in a burial chamber called Tomb of the Leopards at the Etruscan Necropolis of Tarquinii/Tarquinii in Lazio, Italy. 6th century B.C. Right image may be the basin jumping ritual.

Tarquinii, is an ancient city in the Roman province of Viterbo/Viterbi, Lazio, Italy, which was established around the 25th Dynasty probably by Taharqa and the Egyptians around this time. Many artifacts highlight Egyptian or Nubian influence, like the changes from cremation to mummification and the building of tombs depicting false doors. It is possible to assume that the Egyptian priests were aware of the prophecies against the *"Black Land"* and so planted their seeds in Italy.

[61]*In support of the hypothesis of kinship between the races of Europe and America, Gennarelli adduces: (a) the existence of pyramids, (b) labyrinths, (c) mummies and (d) hieroglyphic languages in Egypt, America, and Etruria.*

Etruria around the 6th century B.C. developed wine making, road building, agriculture, metalworking, Egyptian style pyramids and commerce.

Figure 25 Colored family from Cape Town, Kimberley, and Pretoria (South Africa), by Henry Trotter.

---

[61] Ancient and Modern Britons: A Retrospect, Volume 1 by David MacRitchie 1884. Digital Reproduction by Google. Volume III. No. 2 Communicated by C.H.E. Carmichael, M.A

By 300 B.C. the new citizens had developed Classical Latin writing, and eventually gave birth to the Roman Empire. Then Polybius informs us that [62]a *race of black* men governed in the Tyrrhenian region.

If different languages correlate to distinct races, Africans (because of their great genetic diversity) would be expected to have the greatest linguistic distinctions. Incidentally, there are more than 2000 languages spoken in Africa. Afrikaans is the only European language, known to have developed in Africa. A generation after the Egyptians and Ethiopians immigrated into Italy, the new residents may have intermarried and resembled the colored people of South Africa.

Taharqa's story entwines with the prayers of the King of Judah, recorded in the bible as well as the insults from their joint adversary, the king of Assyria, *Sennacherib*. It is one of the greatest displays of the spirit's power to communicate with kings and prophets.

The prayers which were recorded before he assumed the throne revealed that God promised him a blessed and ordered reign.

Before you crowned me you have foretold these to me: a great inundation in my time. The sky was extended for me, being thick and abundant with rain.

Taharqa led a period of peace and prosperity, where the empire flourished. In his sixth year there was abundant rainfall and a large harvest. He also restored existing temples, and built new ones.

After these things, and the establishment thereof, Sennacherib king of Assyria came, and entered into Judah, and encamped against the fenced cities, and thought to win them for himself. 2 Chronicles 32:32

Taharqa came to aide Jerusalem and King <u>Hezekiah</u> in withstanding the siege by the Assyrian King.

The Assyrians issued a threat to the Jews that they should not trust in their God nor their weakened Pharaoh. (2Chronicles 32 tells the entire story)

Thou trustest upon the staff of this bruised reed of Egypt, on which if a man lean, it will go into his hand, and pierce it: So is Pharaoh king of Egypt unto all that trust on him.

Isaiah 37:16-20 records that Hezekiah prayed unto the LORD,

Now therefore, O LORD our God, save us from his hand, that all the kingdoms of the earth may know that thou art the LORD, even thou only.

God responds with displeasure against the Jews, but is provoked by Sennacherib's reproach against him and responds:

Therefore thus saith the LORD concerning the king of Assyria, He shall not come into this city, nor shoot an arrow there, nor come before it with shields, nor cast a bank against it.

By the way that he came, by the same shall he return, and shall not come into this city, saith the LORD.

For I will defend this city to save it for mine own sake, and for my servant David's sake.

Historians believe that the Assyrian soldiers retreated because they fell ill; and there are three separate accounts.

---

[62] The general history of Polybius books 1-17 by Hampton 5th ed - Polybius

Berosus author of Chaldean History said

[63] When Sennacherib was returning from his Egyptian war to Jerusalem: he found his army in danger by a plague, for God had sent pestilential distemper upon his army; and on the very first night of the siege, a hundred fourscore and five thousand were destroyed.

According to Herodotus: a divinely-appointed disaster destroyed the army of Sennacherib, after Ethos prayed to the gods. The gods sent a multitude of field-mice, which devoured all the quivers and bowstrings of the enemy, and ate the thongs by which they managed their shields. This is commemorated in a stone statue of Sethos, with a mouse in his hand, and an inscription to this effect - 'Look on me, and learn to reverence the gods.'

The Lord sent an angel, which cut off all the mighty men of valor, and the leaders and captains in the camp of the king of Assyria. So he returned with shame of face to his own land. 2 Chronicles 32:21

His successor, King Esarhaddon, determined to invade Egypt in 671 BC and defeated Taharqa. Esarhaddon declared:

All Nubians I deported from Egypt, leaving not one left to do homage to me.

Taharqa's Queen and children were carried away to Assyria. A nation's power may have been believed to be tied to their women. Thus the tradition of stealing women, according to Herodotus was a very common practice among the nations.

From Io, the daughter of Argos, Helen from Troy and according to Herodotus: *at a latter period, certain Greeks stole the daughter of Tyre named Europe and carried off Medea from a city of the Colchis.*

Taharqa then prayed for success. His final inscriptions end with a complete reliance on God's help.

Oh, Amun Oh, You who did not abandon what he has created, while it is half realized. You shall hear them for me, and you shall turn back their evil words. Do not let me enter an affair that you hate. Do not let me do what you hate. I am your little child, while it is you who begot, all that comes into being.

Oh Amun, there is no one who gives you orders. It is you that gives orders. That which you say to me: "Go forth, go forth", I shall go forth.

Amun is the omnipotent God of Gods, but also a father who cares for his son, Taharqa and must protect him. So Taharqa was permitted to go forth, and seized control of Egypt as far north as Memphis. Esarhaddon set about returning to Egypt to eject him, but fell ill and died on his way. Taharqa received a sign that his time was ended and retreated to Nubia. The Assyrian leader Ashurbanipal continued to reign.

Now, inspired by the cries of his children, Divine Providence imparts revenge against the Assyrians.

---

[63] The Complete Works of Flavius-Josephus the Celebrated Jewish Historian by William Whiston 1895

The book of the vision of Nahum the Elkoshite.

God is jealous, and the Lord revengeth; the Lord revengeth, and is furious; the Lord will take vengeance on his adversaries, and he reserveth wrath for his enemies.

The Lord is <u>slow to anger, but great in power, and will not at all acquit the wicked</u>: the [Lord hath his way in the whirlwind and in the storm, and the clouds are the dust of his feet.]

Who can stand before his indignation? And who can abide in the fierceness of his anger? His fury is poured out like fire, and the rocks are thrown down by him.

He is good, a strong hold in the day of trouble; and he knoweth them that trust in him.

But <u>with an overrunning flood</u> he will make an utter end of the place thereof, and darkness shall pursue his enemies.

What do ye imagine against the Lord? He will make an utter end: affliction shall not rise up the second time.

the Lord hath given a commandment concerning thee, no more of thy name be sown:

Out of the house of thy gods will I cut off the graven image and the molten image: I will make thy grave; for thou art vile. Nahum 1

The Assyrian Empire collapsed mainly in [64]*consequence of an extraordinary rise of the Tigris, which swept away a portion of the city wall, and so gave admittance to the enemy. Then the Assyrian monarch determined that resistance would be vain, fired his palace and destroyed himself. Nineveh ceased to exist.*

Historians say that the Assyrian Empire which was a rising power, terminated very prematurely, after Asshur-bani-pal in 640 B.C. It was completely erased, leaving nothing behind of its greatness.

Behold upon the mountains the feet of him that bringeth good tidings, that publisheth peace! O Judah, keep thy solemn feasts, perform thy vows: for the wicked shall no more pass through thee; he is utterly cut off. Nahum 1:15

Although Taharqa displayed the ancient humility which empowered all the kings before him, the Nubians were proud and haughty. Their reign in Egypt was no better than the evil pride of the Egyptians. Isaiah foretells a coming disgrace to all Ethiopian people.

---

[64] History of Herodotus, Volume 1 Herodotus Halicarnasseus, George Rawlinson, Henry Creswicke Rawlinson (sir), John Gardner Wilkinson (sir) J. Murray, 1862

Isaiah 18 Prophecy against Cush (New International Version)

Woe to the land of whirring wings, along the rivers of Sudan
which sends envoys by *Sea* in papyrus boats over the water. (Voyages of Hanno)
Go, swift messengers, to a people tall and smooth-skinned, to a people feared far and wide, an aggressive
nation of strange speech, whose land is divided by rivers.
All you people of the world, you who live on the earth, when a banner is raised on the mountains,
you will see it, and when a trumpet sounds, you will hear it.
This is what the Lord says to me:
   "I will remain quiet and will look on from my dwelling place, like shimmering heat in the sunshine,
like a cloud of dew in the heat of harvest."
And the Lord said, like as my servant Isaiah hath walked naked and barefoot three years for a sign and
wonder upon Egypt and upon Ethiopia;
So shall the king of Assyria lead away the Egyptians prisoners, and the Ethiopians captives, young and old,
naked and barefoot, even with their buttocks uncovered, to the shame of Egypt.
And they shall be afraid and ashamed of Ethiopia their expectation, and of Egypt their glory. Isaiah 20:3-5

A Decree against the Ethiopian daughters of Zion.

Figure 26 Nubian woman, Egyptian Sudan 1890

*16 Moreover the Lord saith, because the daughters of Zion are
haughty, and walk with stretched forth necks and wanton eyes,
walking and mincing as they go, and making a tinkling with their feet:
17 Therefore the Lord will smite with a scab the crown of the head of
the daughters of Zion, and the Lord will discover their secret parts.
18 In that day the Lord will take away the bravery of their tinkling
ornaments about their feet, and their cauls, and their round tires like
the moon,
19 The chains, and the bracelets, and the mufflers,
20 The bonnets, and the ornaments of the legs, and the headbands,
and the tablets, and the earrings,
21 The rings, and nose jewels,
22 The changeable suits of apparel, and the mantles, and the
wimples, and the crisping pins,
23 The glasses, and the fine linen, and the hoods, and the veils.
24 And it shall come to pass, that instead of sweet smell there shall be
stink; and instead of a girdle a rent; and instead of well-set hair,
baldness; and instead of a stomacher a girding of sackcloth; and
burning instead of beauty.
25 Thy men shall fall by the sword, and thy mighty in the war.
26 And her gates shall lament and mourn; and she being desolate
shall sit upon the ground. Isaiah 3: 16-26*

After Ezekiel's prophecy, the Carthaginian sailor Hanno, sailed to West Africa with sixty five ships, and about thirty thousand men and women.

These may be the messengers sent in ships to make the careless Ethiopians run from East Africa. Hanno said that they founded cities, on the West coast of Africa and described seeing a fully active volcano and he provides the first record of gorillas. Hanno is believed to have traveled as far South as Zimbabwe. Thus establishing a trade route through the Sahara, connecting the Ethiopians from the East and West. These new settlers may have been a part of flourishing civilizations, like the Nok civilization in Nigeria. Their presence also coincides with the Bantu expansion and the first signs of food production there. Later on Herodotus tells us that these travelers originated from East Africa.

Figure 27A map illustrating the voyage of Hanno the Navigator to West Africa, from the 1837 book The Encyclopædia of Geography, by Hugh Murray

[65] *For the areas between the equatorial rain forest and Lake Victoria, still a third agency of the spread of food production can be proposed, the expansion of Central Sudanic-speaking peoples. Loanwords from Central Sudanic peoples, who were already food producers by 300BC. African modes of food production were spread to the far southern tip of the continent. The agents generally recognized in this process have been the Early Iron Age Bantu.*

Hanno, said that the Garamantes of the Niger region, used four-horse chariots, to hunt the Ethiopians who could out run horses, and were swifter on foot than any nation in the world. Half a century earlier Jeremiah recorded a message, which corresponds to Hanno's description of the Ethiopians he encountered in West Africa.

If thou hast run with the footmen, and they have wearied thee, then how canst thou contend with horses?
Jeremiah 12:5

Civilization finally exits the African garden. This ends the era of the woman and the serpent, and the word is disseminated into branches of Art, Theology, and Science, while magic and the occult are driven underground. They eventually become the guarded secrets of lodges and secret societies.

Ezekiel 622-570 BC prophesized that Egypt would become *the basest of Kingdoms; neither shall it exalt itself anymore above the nations. 29:15 messengers shall go forth from God in ships to make the careless Ethiopians afraid, and great pain shall come upon them, as in the day of Egypt. 30:9…. the land will be sold to the wicked and inhabited by strangers; 30:12 and the pomp of her strength shall cease in her: as for her, a cloud shall cover her, and her daughters shall go into captivity.30:18. And I will scatter the Egyptians among the nations, and disperse them throughout the countries. 30:23*

---

[65] From Hunters to Farmers: The Causes and Consequences of Food Production in Africa. John Desmond Clark, Steven A. Brandt. University of California Press, Jan 1, 1984 pg33

Isaiah says that "The Lord will stir up Egyptian against Egyptian—brother will fight against brother, neighbor against neighbor, city against city, kingdom against kingdom.

This was fulfilled by the 26th Dynasty pharaohs Psamtik I & II from 664-610 & 595-589 BC.

In an effort to take control of the throne against the other possible heirs [66]*Psammeticus hired soldiers out of Arabia, Caria, and Ionia, and in a field near the city Memphis, he got the day. Some of the kings of the other side were slain, and the rest fled into Africa, and were not able to further contend for the Kingdom.*

Psammeticus now having gained possession of the whole... bestowed likewise upon his mercenary soldiers many large rewards over and above their pay promised them. Being therefore that he had gained the kingdom by the help of his stipendiary soldiers, he entrusted them chiefly in the concerns of the government, and entertained great numbers of strangers and foreigners.

Afterwards undertaking an expedition into Syria, (to honor the foreigners), he placed them in the right wing of his army; but out of slight disregard for the natural Egyptians, he drew them up in the left; with which affront the Egyptians were so incensed, that above two hundred thousand of them revolted, and marched away towards Ethiopia, there to settle themselves in new habitations.

Psammeticus was kind and liberal to all strangers that came into Egypt... and was the first of all the kings of Egypt that encouraged foreigners to traffic in his country.

His daughter was then selected to be trained as God's wife.

***In that day five cities in Egypt will speak the language of Canaan** and swear allegiance to the Lord Almighty. One of them will be called *the City of the Sun. (NIV) Isaiah 19:18*

The people inhabiting along the sides of the Nile, from Syene to Meroe, are not Ethiopians, but Arabians, who for the sake of fresh water approached the Nile, and there dwelt: as also that *the City of the Sun, which we said before in the description of Egypt, standeth not far from Memphis, was founded by the Arabians.
Pliny chapter 29 The Gulf of the Red Sea.

Pliny tries to explain how the Arabians got to Egypt, because they are not Ethiopian or dark skinned. Some believed at the time that Arabia extended into the east coast of the Nile, but he believed that they got there because they were looking for fresh water. The Egyptian language was also completely erased and replaced with the language of Canaan, Arabic.

In the 16th century geographer Johannes Leo Africanus, 1494 – 1554 travelled throughout Africa and gives us the first pre-colonial portrait of the country, he says:
[67]

---

[66] The Historical Library of Diodorus the Sicilian: In Fifteen Books. To which are Added the Fragments of Diodorus, and Those Published by H. Valesius, I. Rhodomannus, & F. Ursinus, translated by G Booth ESQ Harvard College Library In two volumes. Vol. 1 byDiodorus (Siculus.)Chapter 5 pg. 69-71
[67] A Dictionary of the English Language: in Two Volumes, Volume 2 Noah Webster, Black and Young, 1832

[68] *The country people are of a swart and browne color: but the citizens are white. Neither are there left any true Egyptians, besides a few Christians, which are at present remaining. The residue have mingled themselves amongst the Arabians and Moors.*

(Schwarz is also German for black)

SWARTH'INESS, *n.* Tawniness; a dusky or dark complexion.

SWARTH'Y, *a.* [See *Swart*.] Being of a dark hue or dusky complexion; tawny. In warm climates, the complexion of men is universally *swarthy* or black. The Moors, Spaniards and Italians are more *swarthy* than the French, Germans and English.

> Their *swarthy* hosts would darken all our plains. *Addison.*

2. Black; as, the *swarthy* African.

A Decree against the Jews.

25 But Hezekiah rendered not again according to the benefit done unto him; for [his heart was lifted up]: therefore there was wrath upon him, and upon Judah and Jerusalem.
The lord destroys the proud and boastful, he brings to shame and humiliation those who insult him. So he inflicted the king with an illness.
26 *Notwithstanding Hezekiah humbled himself for the pride of his heart, both he and the inhabitants of Jerusalem, so that the wrath of the LORD came not upon them in the days of Hezekiah.*
27 *And Hezekiah had exceeding much riches and honor: and he made himself treasuries for silver, and for gold, and for precious stones, and for spices, and for shields, and for all manner of pleasant jewels;*
2 Chronicles 32:25-27

2 Kings 20:12-14
[12] *At that time Berodachbaladan, the son of Baladan, king of Babylon, sent letters and a present unto Hezekiah: for he had heard that Hezekiah had been sick.*
[13] *And Hezekiah hearkened unto them, and shewed them all the house of his precious things, the silver, and the gold, and the spices, and the precious ointment, and all the house of his armor, and all that was found in his treasures: there was nothing in his house, nor in all his dominion, that Hezekiah shewed them not.*
[14] *Then came Isaiah the prophet unto King Hezekiah, and said unto him, what said these men? And from whence came they unto thee? And Hezekiah said, they are come from a far country, even from Babylon.*
[15] *And he said, what have they seen in thine house? And Hezekiah answered, All the things that are in mine house have they seen: there is nothing among my treasures that I have not shewed them.*
[16] *And Isaiah said unto Hezekiah, Hear the word of the Lord.*
[17] *Behold, the days come, that all that is in thine house, and that which thy fathers have laid up in store unto this day, shall be carried into Babylon: nothing shall be left, saith the Lord.*

---

[68] The History and Description of Africa: And of the Notable Things Therein Contained Leo (Africanus), Robert Brown, John Pory Hakluyt Society, 1896 pg856-857

Just three generations later, Josiah the great grandson of Hezekiah was noted as one of the most righteous kings. *And like unto him was there no king before him, that turned to the Lord with all his heart, and with all his soul, and with all his might, according to all the laws of Moses; neither after him arose there any like him.* 2 Kings 23:25

But: 29 In his days Pharaoh Necho king of Egypt, went up against the king of Assyria to the river Euphrates: and king Josiah went against him;
Josiah was righteous, but ignorant of the fact, that he was fighting the very people who had been allies to his grandfather. By doing this, he inadvertently sided with, the enemy of God.
My people are destroyed for lack of Knowledge. Hosea 4:6
In those days the features of the Israelite population were changing; so there were many more as fair as the
> Assyrians than the dark skinned Egyptians.
> Daniel begs an explanation for the rapid change of features among his people.
> *O Lord, righteousness is unto thee, but unto us confusion of faces, as at this day; to the men of Judah, and to the inhabitants of Jerusalem, and unto all Israel, that are near, and that are far off, through all the countries whither thou hast driven them, because of their sin that they have trespassed against thee.*
> *O Lord, to us belongeth confusion of face, to our kings, to our princes, and to our fathers, because we have sinned against thee. Therefore the curse is poured upon us.* Daniel 9:7-8 &11
> Daniel tries to explain these changes as a curse of the plague; and these emerging differences among the people is counteracted with new rituals of passing their children through the fire. Ezekiel tells us that the Israelites did all they could to retain this idealized darkness of the Egyptians:
> *they did not every man cast away the abominations of their eyes, neither did they forsake the idols of Egypt. And they caused to pass through the fire all that openeth the womb.* Ezekiel 20:8 & 26
> But God removes the stigma once attached to it, and reiterates that these people have been made clean and purified and many more shall be made white. Daniel 12:10 and 11:35

21 But Necho sent ambassadors to him, saying:
"What have I to do with thee, thou king of Judah? I come not against thee this day, but against the house wherewith I have war: for God commanded me to make haste: forbear thee from meddling with God, who is with me, that he destroy thee not."
22 Nevertheless, Josiah would not turn his face from him, but disguised himself, that he might fight with him, and hearkened not unto the words of Necho from the mouth of God, and came to fight in the valley of Megiddo. 2 Chronicles 35:21-23

This belief that God was still with the Egyptians caused Egypt and the Pharaohs to be idolized by the Jews. After so many generations in shackles they could not release their spirit from its former yoke. They wanted a king like the Egyptians and instituted their own orders, but never learnt complete reliance on their unseen God. They needed to see him, they needed a sign, so Isaiah prophesized that:
> *Therefore the Lord himself shall give you a sign; Behold, a virgin shall conceive, and bear a son, and shall call his name Immanuel.* Isaiah 7:14

They waited on this king, but tired of waiting. Their hope may have been renewed by their righteous Josiah. His death brought about a spiraling disbelief in the God of Israel; which Jeremiah recorded in his lamentations.

Both the Israelites and Ethiopians who had utterly relied on their divine guide, and intimately known and worshiped him, would soon become outcasts, perpetual slaves, despised and rejected by men.

God speaks his long term Plan into the heart of his people.

8 Therefore wait ye upon me, saith the Lord, until that day that I rise up to the prey: for my determination is to gather the nations, that I may assemble the kingdoms, to pour upon them mine indignation, even all my fierce anger: for all the earth shall be devoured with the fire of my jealousy.
9 For then will I turn to the people a pure language that they may all call upon the name of the Lord, to serve him with one consent.
10 From beyond the rivers of Ethiopia my suppliants, the daughter of my dispersed, shall bring my offering.
11 In that day shalt thou not be ashamed for all thy doings, wherein thou hast transgressed against me: for then I will take away out of the midst of thee them that rejoice in thy pride, and thou shalt no more be haughty because of my holy mountain.
12 I will leave in the midst of thee an afflicted and poor people, and they shall trust in the name of the Lord.
13 The remnant of Israel shall not do iniquity, nor speak lies; neither shall a deceitful tongue be found in their mouth: for they shall feed and lie down, and none shall make them afraid.
14 Sing, O daughter of Zion; shout, O Israel; be glad and rejoice with all the heart, O daughter of Jerusalem.
15 The Lord hath taken away thy judgments, he hath cast out thine enemy: the king of Israel, even the Lord, is in the midst of thee: thou shalt not see evil any more.
16 In that day it shall be said to Jerusalem, Fear thou not: and to Zion, Let not thine hands be slack.
17 The Lord thy God in the midst of thee is mighty; he will save, he will rejoice over thee with joy; he will rest in his love, he will joy over thee with singing.
18 I will gather them that are sorrowful for the solemn assembly, who are of thee, to whom the reproach of it was a burden.
19 Behold, at that time I will undo all that afflict thee: and I will save her that halteth, and gather her that was driven out; and I will get them praise and fame in every land where they have been put to shame.
20 At that time will I bring you again, even in the time that I gather you: for I will make you a name and a praise among all people of the earth, when I turn back your captivity before your eyes, saith the Lord.
Zephaniah 3 (640–609BC.)

Daniel 623 BC to-Mid 6thC.

The bible at this point has received many prophetic and historic contributions, including Moses' five books from Genesis to Deuteronomy, the records of his successor Joshua, the records of the Judges, and prophets and the chronicles of the Kings which comprise the words of the prophets during the reign of each King. These were all recorded by the divine and sacred duties of the scribes. These prophets recorded the warnings of God, to illustrate the future of all the Kingdoms of the Earth and the prophetic direction which they are ordained to follow.

The prophet Daniel's visions covered the succeeding 2500 years of earth history. This led him to believe that there would be several generations, before the word of God spoken through Zephaniah would be realized. This long period also serves as the breakdown of the haughty and proud spirit of the Ethiopians. This vast space of time is illustrated as *"The Man"* which represents the succeeding kingdoms and governments which would dominate the world, until the *gathering of the nations.*

"The Man"

Daniel was placed in Babylon and schooled among the Babylonians. From then on the Empire began to rise. Babylonian King, Nebuchadnezzar, invaded Judah and began a siege of Jerusalem about 589 BC. Their forces broke down the walls of Jerusalem, then plundered and burnt the city. Most of the Jews were taken captive to Babylon.

During this time, Nebuchadnezzar had a dream which he could not recall. He searched for an oracle among all of his people but found none.

After the fall of Egypt and the disappearance of Assyria, it was clear that there was a superior spirit guiding the events along. The kings which followed all sort their own oracles and tried to find out what this divine Providence was.

Daniel was appointed to reveal this dream.

Thou, O king, sawest, and behold a great image. This great image, whose brightness was excellent, stood before thee; and the form thereof was terrible. This image's head was of fine gold, his breast and his arms of silver, his belly and his thighs of brass, his legs of iron, his feet part of iron and part of clay. Thou sawest till that a rock was cut out without hands, which smote the image upon his feet that were of iron and clay, and break them to pieces. Then was the iron, the clay, the brass, the silver, and the gold, broken to pieces together, and the rock that smote the image became a great mountain, and filled the whole earth. Daniel 2:31-35

Daniel's interpretation of this vision: *Thou art this head of gold. And after thee shall arise another kingdom inferior to thee, and another third kingdom of brass, which shall bear rule over all the earth. And the fourth kingdom shall be strong as iron: forasmuch as iron breaketh in pieces and subdueth all things: and as iron that breaketh all these, shall it break in pieces and bruise.* Daniel 2:38-40

The kingdom of Babylon represents the head of Gold from 606-539 BC

20 But when "his heart was lifted up," (Nebuchadnezzar) and his mind hardened in pride, he was deposed from his kingly throne, and they took his glory from him:

21 And he was driven from the sons of men; and his heart was made like the beasts, and his dwelling was with the wild asses: they fed him with grass like oxen, and his body was wet with the dew of heaven; till he knew that the most high God ruled in the kingdom of men, and that he appointeth over it whomsoever he will. Daniel 5:20-21

Thus shall Babylon sink *and never rise again.* Jeremiah 51:64

Jeremiah 650-570 BC

The Nabonidus (Nabunaid) Chronicle a stone document discovered in ruins near the city of Baghdad in 1879 dates the fall of Babylon to 539 B.C. This is just thirty years after the death and prophecy of Jeremiah.

Daniel (10:1-13) says that *in the third year of Cyrus king of Persia...* The angel Gabriel visited Daniel, *but the prince of the kingdom of Persia withstood him one and twenty days: but, lo, Michael, one of the chief princes, came to help me; and I remained there with the kings of Persia.*

It seems that Cyrus was preparing to invade Babylon and was invoking divine guidance. Cyrus is also described as the *Anointed One, w*ho is given the responsibility to restore the temple and free the Jews. History then informs us of the other kingdoms. 2Chronicles 36:18-21

Figure 28 Croesus at the stake. 500–490 BC. From en: Vulci. Louvre Museum Department of Greek, Etruscan and Roman Antiquities, Sully, 1st floor, room 43, case 19 Durand Collection, 1836

Croesus king of Lydia (595 BC – 546 BC) is mentioned here because he was one of the wealthiest kings of this era. He dispatched messengers to test the oracles of the region but none satisfied him besides the oracle at Delphi of Greece.

[69]*After this Croesus, having resolved to propitiate the Delphic god with magnificent sacrifices. The messengers who had the charge of conveying these treasures to the shrines, received instructions to ask the oracles whether Croesus should go to war with the Persians and if so, whether he should strengthen himself by the forces of an ally.*

The reply:
If Croesus attacked the Persians, he would destroy a mighty empire.
At the receipt of these oracular replies Croesus was overjoyed, and feeling sure now that he would destroy the empire of the Persians, Croesus a third time consulted the oracle... The question whereto he now desired an answer was- "Whether his kingdom would be of long duration?" The following was the reply of the Pythoness:-
Wait till the time shall come when a mule is monarch of Media; Then, thou delicate Lydian, away to the pebbles of Hermus; Haste, oh! haste thee away, nor blush to behave like a coward.

---

[69] History of Herodotus, Volume 1 Herodotus Halicarnasseus, George Rawlinson, Henry Creswicke Rawlinson (sir), John Gardner Wilkinson (sir) J. Murray, 1862

Of all the answers that had reached him, this pleased him far the best, for it seemed incredible that a mule should ever come to be king of the Medes, and so he concluded that the sovereignty would never depart from himself or his seed after him.

But Herodotus says that:

Cyrus of Persia was that mule. For the parents of Cyrus were of different races, and of different conditions-his mother a Midian princess, daughter of King Astyages, and his father a Persian and a subject, who though so far beneath her in all respects, had married his royal mistress.

Furthermore the kingdom which the oracle predicted to fall if he attacked the Persians was his own.

Thus saith the Lord to his anointed, to Cyrus, whose right hand I have holden, to subdue nations before him; and I will *loose the loins of kings, to open before him the two leaved gates; and the gates shall not be shut;* Isaiah 45:1

Cyrus was given the responsibility to bring the Jews out of Babylon so that they could build their temple.

And the elders of the Jews built, and prospered through the prophesying of Haggai the prophet and

Zechariah the son of Iddo (520-440 B.C).

And they built, and finished it, according to the commandment of the God of Israel, and according to the commandment of Cyrus, and Darius, and Artaxerxes kings of Persia.

15 And this house was finished on the third day of the month Adar, which was in the sixth year of the reign of Darius the king.

16 And the children of Israel, the priests, and the Levites, and the rest of the children of the captivity, kept the dedication of this house of God with joy. **Ezra (480–400 BC)** *6: 14-16*

Figure 29 a). Miniature 12 from the 14thC Constantine Manasses Chronicle, Kings of Persia Cambyses, and Gyges: b).Darius Winged sphinx from Darius' palace at Susa, c).soldiers the immortals.

By the grace of Ahuramazda I built this palace. The men who adorned the wall, those were Mides and Egyptians. Darius King of Persia

Persian theology was based on the teachings of Zarathustra. Zoroastrianism is very similar to Jewish teachings, in that they worship one God. Zarathustra recognized Satan as the enemy of divine order and truth and the leader of demons which he called *"The Lie"*; and God as Ahura-mazda.

Cambyses II was the eldest son of King Cyrus II the Great. He ruled from 529–522 BC, and conquered Egypt in 525 during the reign of Psamtik III. Many of the soldiers in his army may have been those who deflected from Egypt.

But while in Egypt, Cambyses planned expeditions against the Kingdom of Kush (located in what is now the Republic of Sudan), the Oasis of Amon (modern Wāḥat Sīwah), and Carthage.

[70]*Herodotus reports, in his own voice, a story about Cambyses, ruler of Persia, who planned aggressive campaigns against Egyptians, Ethiopians and Carthaginians. Cambyses ordered his navy to sail against Carthage. The Phoenicians, however refused to comply.*
He [71]*was prevented from executing his project, because the Phoenicians, who composed his maritime force, persevered in refusing to be employed against a nation which was descended from the same ancestors.*

Phoenicia was the area from Lebanon in the Middle East, to Armenia and Georgia, and Herodotus says that the people in this area came from the Eritrean Sea. Isaiah said that they sent envoys in papyrus boats out to sea. These long voyages may be the voyages of Hanno, to West Africa, and the thousands of people who were left to settle in this region which is sometimes referred to as Western Sudan.

---

[70] Rethinking the Other in Antiquity Erich S. Gruen Princeton University Press, Aug 27, 2012 Pg. 118
[71]The Voyage of Hanno: Translated, and Accompanied with the Greek Text, Explained from the Accounts of Modern Travellers, Defended Against the Objections of Mr. Dodwell and Other Writers, and Illustrated by Maps from Ptolemy, D'Anville, and Bougainville Hanno, Thomas Falconer by T. Cadell Jun. and Davies, 1797 page 86

1. According to the Persians best informed in history, the Phœnicians began the quarrel. This people, who had formerly dwelt on the shores of the Erythræan Sea,[2] having migrated to the Mediterranean and settled in the parts which they now inhabit, began at once, they say, to adventure on long voyages, [72] freighting their vessels with the wares of Egypt and Assyria.[3]

The editor of these works of Herodotus says this:

[7] The commentators have found some difficulty in showing why the Colchians should have been held responsible for an outrage committed by the Phœnicians, and have been obliged to suggest that it was merely owing to their equally belonging to the comity of Asiatic nations; but the traditions of mutual responsibility are more readily explained by our remembering that there was perhaps an ethnic relationship between the two nations, Colchis in the time of the Argonauts being peopled by the same Cushite or (so called) Æthiopian race, which in the remote age of Inachus, and before the arrival of the Semites in Syria, held the seaboard of Phœnicia. The primitive Medes would seem to have been one of the principal divisions of the great Cushite or Scythic race, their connexion with Colchis and Phœnicia being marked by the myth of *Medea* in one [73] quarter, and of Andro*meda* in the other.

Cushite or Scythic, literally means Black or White so it must therefore be one or the other. These are the simple errors which have been injected into history and have virtually changed the story.

Xerxes I later embarked on costly wars against Greece (484-481 BC) in the battles of Artemisium and Salamis.

---

[72] History of Herodotus, Volume 1 page 121 Herodotus Halicarnasseus, George Rawlinson, Henry Creswicke Rawlinson (sir), John Gardner Wilkinson
[73] Editor's conclusions recorded in the foot Note: History of Herodotus, Volume 1 page 123 Herodotus Halicarnasseus, George Rawlinson, Henry Creswicke Rawlinson (sir), John Gardner Wilkinson

Historian Jean-Louis Huot says that there has been much speculation on the real causes for the expedition.

They could not have been economic, because Greece was not important then. [74]But Herodotus tells us that the *Persians traced their very ancient enmity towards the Greeks to their attack upon Troy in the Trojan wars. This happened after the Persians stole the Grecian princess Helen and the Grecians in turn destroyed Troy.*

The invasion of Greece has been considered the cause of the decline of the Achaemenid/Persian Empire; but this empire was also plagued with internal discord, from the threat of contenders always prepared to assassinate a king, to usurp the throne.

From 405 to 358 BC, Xerxes reigned after his father Darius II and married Jewish Queen Esther. Esther 1:1 says that *Xerxes ruled over 127 provinces stretching from India to Kush.* The Zorastrian faith was still in full force during Xerxes' reign.

Xerxes proclaimed:

Among these countries (in rebellion) there was one where, previously, Daevas had been worshipped. Afterward, through Ahura Mazda's favor, I destroyed this sanctuary of Daevas and proclaimed, "Let Daevas not be worshipped" There, where Daevas had been worshipped before, I worshipped Ahura Mazda.

Buddha was born during this time. His mother, Queen Maya, dreamt that an elephant entered into her, on the night that he was conceived. Buddha's preaching's significantly detracted from the most ancient texts of his people, the *Veda* doctrines of Polytheism. This may have been due to the pressures of the Persian rulers.

Figure 30 a). A Chinese silken banner probably used during the reign of the first emperor Qin Shi Huang. Excavated from a tomb at Changsha, Hunan province, dated to the Western Han Dynasty (252 BC – 9 AD). Scanned from Michael Sullivan's The Arts of China: Fourth Edition (1999)
b). The Terracotta Army or the "Terra Cotta Warriors and Horses", is a collection of terracotta sculptures depicting the armies of Qin Shi Huang, the first Emperor of China. Image by Immanuel Giel
c). Paintings from 121 BC- 8th century AD, in the Mogao Caves, or the Caves of the Thousand Buddhas. There are 492 temples 25 km (16 mi) southeast of the center of Dunhuang, a Gansu province, China.
d). 8th century fresco at Mogao Caves near Dunhuang in Gansu Province. Depiction of the Han Emperor Wu worshiping statues of the Buddha. Located in Cave 323 in Mogao. With the departure of Zhang Qian to Western lands 8th century Reproduction in Roderick Whitfield, Susan Whitfield, Neville Agnew, and Lois Conner, Cave Temples of Mogao: Art and History on the Silk Road. Getty Conservation Institute and the J. Paul Getty Museum, 2000. ISBN 0892365854
e) Ganeśa, Cambodia, 2nd half of the 10th century CE. sandstone.

He established a renewed emphasis on a perpetual state of nirvana which continued, often endangered but mostly intact. The entire Asian continent recluses within the great stone walls and try

---

[74] Larcher's Notes on Herodotus: Historical and Critical Remarks on, Volume 1 page 421-425 By Pierre Henri Larcher 1829

throughout history to keep invaders out. They avoid most cycles of domination and subjugation and represent one of the few elephants in the story, until the 19th century, when a combination of factors like plagues or epidemics, famines, earthquakes and European invasions decimated the population of Indians and Asians; and created a temporary opening for European colonialism.

According to Herodotus the Asians of his day (400 BC.) were as dark as Aethiopians/Ethiopians but with straight hair. How, when and why did some Asians lose their pigmentation? Will be answered with a few more clues; but it is worthwhile to note that almost all Asians, including Chinese, Vietnamese, Taiwanese and Javanese, people still exhibited darker complexions as late as the end of the 19th century.

Figure 31 Nordisk familjebok by Bernhard Meijer Herakles publishing, early 1900s An Ethnographic Portrait of the Ancient World

1. *Kosack. (Cossacks)*
2. *Samojed. (Samoyedic peoples)*
3. *Ostjak. (Ostyak peoples)*
4. *Tungus. (Tungusic peoples)*
5. *Tsjuktsjer. (Chukchi people)*
6. *Giljakiska. (Nivkh people or Gilyak)*
7. *Kamtsjadal. (Itelmens or Kamchadal)*

8. *Aino. (Ainu people)*
9. *Kabardin. (Kabarday or Kabardin people)*
10. *Tsjerkess. (Adyghe people or Circassians)*
11. *Kirgis. (Kyrgyz people)*
12. *Burjät. (Buryats)*
13. *Golder. (Nanai people, formerly known as Golds or Samagir)*
14. *Korean. (Koreans)*
15. *Japan och japanska. (Japanese people or Yamato people)*

16. *Georgiska. (Georgian people)*
17. *Kalmuckiska. (Kalmyk people)*
18. *Kines. (Chinese people)*
19. *Japan och japanska.*
    (Japanese people or Yamato people)

20. *Tatar. (Tatars)*
21. *Jude. (Jews)*
22. *Perser. (Persian people)*
23. *Belutsjer. (Baloch people)*
24. *Lao. (Lao people)*
25. *Dajak (Borneo). (Dayak people)*
26. *Negrito. (Negrito peoples)*
27. *(Indigenous people of Sulawesi or Celebes)*

28. *Arab. (Arab people)*
29. *Vedda (på Ceylon). (Vedda people)*
30. *Singales. (Sinhalese people)*
31. *Indier. (Indian people)*
32. *Bata (Sumatra). (Batak people)*
33. *Bataviska. (Betawi people, named after Batavia, Dutch East Indies)*
34. *Javan. (Javanese people)* 35. *Sundanska. (Sundanese people)*

[75]In 317 BC. Sir Smith says that a general census of Attica, by Demetrius Phalereus, noted that there were 21,000 citizens, 10,000 metics and 400,000 slaves (there may have been many Indians or Colchis, we can infer from Agesilaus, King of Sparta Greece from 400-360 BC)

[76]*One day he ordered his commissaries to sell the prisoners, but to strip them first. Their clothes found many purchasers: but as to the prisoners themselves, their skins being soft and white, by reason of their having lived so much within doors, the spectators only laughed at them, thinking they would be of no service as slaves. Whereon Agesilaus, who stood by at the auction, said to his troops, these are the people whom you fight with* (against*); and then pointing to the rich spoils, those are the things ye fight for.*

The prophet Joel 400-360 3:6 says

The children of Judah and the children of Jerusalem were also sold unto the Grecians.

[77]*the Egyptian priests, out of their sacred records relate, that Orpheus, Musaeus, Melampodes, Daedalus, Homer the poet, Lycurgus the Spartan, Solon the Athenian, Plato the philosopher, Pythagoras the Samian, Eudoxus the mathematician, Democritus the Abderite, and Cenopides the Chian, all came to them in Egypt, and they show certain marks and signs of all these being there. Of some by pictures; and others, by their names. And they bring arguments from every that is used, to prove that everything wherein the Grecians excel, and for which they are admired, was brought over from Egypt into Greece. pg95*

These include *their religious rites, fables; in Greece, of Egyptian extraction and the exquisite art of the Stone-carvers in Egypt.* (Heading of page *89*)

Figure 32 Sacrifice of Conon. Temple of the Palmyrene Gods in Dura-Europos. 1

Diodorus also says that: *Letters came out of Phoenicia into Greece and Phoenicians were the overseers of the sacred mysteries from Egypt,* so that the priests were selected exclusively from members of their families. Thus Grecian religious ceremonies and deities were copies of Egyptian worship and essentially the reenactment of the ancient culture of the Egyptians.

---

[75] In the Dictionary of Greek and Roman Geography, Volume 1 edited by Sir William Smith in 1872 page 262 V. Extent and Population.

[76] Plutarch, page 276 Volume 4 by A. J. Valpy, 1832 by Plutarch

[77] The Historical Library of Diodorus the Sicilian: In Fifteen Books. To which are Added the Fragments of Diodorus, and Those Published by H. Valesius, I. Rhodomannus, & F. Ursinus, translated by G Booth ESQ Harvard College Library In two volumes. Vol. 1 printed by W.M Dowall 1814 by Diodorus (Siculus.) pg89 &95 pg. 336

Figure 33 a). Athenian politician and General, Themistocles (524–459 BC) image by livius.org b). Philip II of Macedon father of Alexander threat Victory medal (niketerion) struck in Tarsus, 2nd century BC. C). [78]Earliest known Image of Aristotle right tutoring Alexander the Great to the left d). Marble head of Alexander the Great (325-300 BC). From the Archaeological Museum, Pella, Central Macedonia, Greece by Vlas2000 e). Bronze bust looks like Alexander but has been attributed to Ptolemy I believed to be the half-brother of Alexander from Phillip's concubine Arisone (ca. 367-283 BC) Walters-museum

Greece maintained the Persian doctrines, but continued in Egyptian paganism. Greek mythology, morphed the imaginary with reality and told their history in the most dramatic and memorable ways. One of their stories *Andromeda, seems like* a historical tale of a white woman, born to Ethiopians.

Themistocles (524–459 BC) is considered a founder of the Athenian Empire. He was an illegitimate child who became one of the *strategoi* or generals elected to Rule in 493 BC. His decisive defeat of the more numerous Persians, marked a turning point in the Greco-Persian Wars. Historians say that [79]*the significance of these Greek victories is nearly incalculable...*This ensured that *Greek political forms and intellectual concepts would be handed down to latter societies.*

From 330-168 BC Greece remained the *Helen* of the East while Phoenicia claimed the Western territory of Carthage in North Africa in the loins of our Statue.

Greece continued to grow, until Alexander the Great formally ushered in the era of Grecian power. Alexander's mother dreamt that her womb was struck by a thunder bolt, causing a flame that spread "far and wide" before dying away. His father, Philip also saw himself, in a dream, securing his wife's womb with a seal engraved with a lion's image. Alexander used these legends to show that he was superhuman and destined for greatness from conception.

When Alexander was thirteen, his father hired Aristotle, to tutor him. In return, Philip agreed to rebuild Aristotle's hometown of Stageira, which he had destroyed. Phillip also repopulated it by freeing its ex-citizens who had been taken as slaves. [80]Aristotle taught Alexander medicine, philosophy, morals, religion, logic, and art; but also educated him on the secrets of power. These secrets had been handed down for centuries as oral tradition probably carried by kings and priests from the fallen kingdoms. This instruction reinforced Alexander's belief that he was a divine being and declared that he too was son of God. Aristotle, so incensed and infuriated, made his secrets public and stirred Alexander to rage. Alexander's letter to Aristotle.

---

[78] From page 2784 fol.96 'Animals and their uses' by Ibn Bakhtishu. British Museum copied by Bridgeman Art Library.
[79] Western Society: A Brief History, Volume 1: From Antiquity to Enlightenment. Page 50-51 John P. McKay, Bennett D. Hill, John Buckler, Clare Haru Crowston, Merry E. Wiesner-Hanks Publisher Macmillan, 2010 ISBN 0312594283,
[80] The Anabasis of Alexander, Or, The History of the Wars and Conquests of Alexander the Great
Arrian Hodder and Stoughton, 1884 – Iran pg. 8 chpt 1 bk1.

[81] You have not done well to publish your books of oral doctrine; for what is there now that we excel others in, if those things which we have been particularly instructed in be laid open to all? For my part, I assure you, I had rather excel others in the knowledge of what is excellent, than in the extent of my power and dominion. Farewell.

Alexander ascended the throne at age twenty after the death of his father in 336 B.C. His expedition to conquer the world led him to success against the Persians and their vast empire. When he arrived in Jerusalem, Josephus said that the Jews surrendered, and showed him the prophecy recorded in Daniel chapter 8: 20-27, which described a mighty Grecian king who would conquer the Persian Empire.

He took Tyre, a formidable nation in the Gaza region of Lebanon, East of Egypt. Then founded a capital in Egypt called Alexandria. He returned a brief period of the old splendor to Egypt, where he was regarded as a liberator, and crowned the new "master of the Universe" and son of Zeus-Ammon.

15 Thou wast perfect in thy ways from the day thou wast created, till iniquity was found in thee.

16 therefore I will cast thee as profane out of the mountain of God: and I will destroy thee, O covering cherub, from the midst of the stones of fire.

17 Thine heart was lifted up because of thy beauty, thou hast corrupted thy wisdom by reason of thy brightness: I will cast thee to the ground, I will lay thee before kings, so they may behold thee.

18 Thou hast defiled thy sanctuaries by the multitude of thine iniquities, by the iniquity of thy traffick; therefore will I bring forth a fire from the midst of thee, it shall devour thee, and I will bring thee to ashes upon the earth in the sight of all them that behold thee.

19 All they that know thee among the people shall be astonished at thee: thou shalt be a terror, and never shalt thou be any more. Ezekiel 28

The cause of Alexander's death continues to mystify; but it is noted that he had the symptoms of fever, thus a *fire came from the midst* of him. Then God says: *I will bring thee to ashes upon the earth in the sight of all them that behold thee.* [82]The remains of Great Alexander laid in plain view in Alexandria when the tenth Ptolemy, replaced his gold sarcophagus with a glass one.

[83]After Alexander's death Ptolemy I obtained the kingdom of Egypt which he transmitted to his descendants. After a distinguished reign of thirty eight years, (323–285) He abdicated the throne to his youngest son, Ptolemy Philadelphus. He survived this event two years and died in B.C 283

The Ptolemic dynasty managed to hold on to Egypt for a number of years, although:

[84]The Nubians regained part of Upper Egypt around 200 BC. The greatest contender for control of Egypt was the Roman Republic, which was conquering most of the Mediterranean lands between the third and first centuries. During the last century BC. the Ptolemies came to depend on Rome to protect them against their other enemies. Only under Queen Cleopatra VII (r. 47-30 BC) did Egypt become a Roman colony.

[81] Fox, Robin Lane (1980). The Search for Alexander. Little Brown & Co. Boston.

[82] The Library of Alexandria: Centre of Learning in the Ancient World, Revised/ By Roy Malcolm MacLeod, Roy MacLeod I.B.Tauris.

[83] The Anabasis of Alexander, Or, The History of the Wars and Conquests of Alexander the Great Arrian Hodder and Stoughton, 1884 – Iran preface

[84] A Brief History of Egypt, by Arthur Goldschmidt, Jr. Infobase Publishing, Jan 1, 2008 pg. 34

Figure 34 a).Bust of Ptolemy I (367-283 BC) founder of the Ptolemaic dynasty in Egypt. Walters Art Museum Acquired 1913 b). Ptolemaic Queen (Brooklyn Museum) Cleopatra VII - 305 and 30 BC Charles Edwin Wilbour Fund by Paul Edmund Stanwick (2002) Portraits of the Ptolemies: Egyptian pharaohs, University of Texas Press, pp. 124-125 c). Ptolemaios X (reign 110-88 BC).; Neues Museum d).Berlin, Germany; Inv.-Nr. 14079 By Anagoria CC-BY-3.0 d) Egyptian and Greek Granodiorite sculpture of the Hellenistic Period (331-30 BC Walters Art Museum Charles Edwin Wilbour Fund by Paul Edmund Stanwick (2002) Portraits of the Ptolemies: as Egyptian pharaohs, University of Texas Press, pp. 124-125). e). Marble statue head with stucco, probably Ptolemy IX. Late 2nd/early 1st century B.C. Originally found at Memphis in Egypt, now residing in the Museum of Fine Arts, Boston. By Keith Schengili-Roberts CC-BY-SA-2.5

At the end of the the 3rd century, Gauls descended on Macedonia; and some even crossed into Asia. This also coincides with the first known mention of the term Albino or Albion in ancient record.

[85]*Lebanon is a Hebrew word meaning white, like Alpes. It was so called on account of its white cliffs, just as Britain is called by Aristotle* (384 to 322BC), *Albion, the Celtic for white.* [86]*It may be stretched from a Phoenician word, "Alben" which signifies white. . The first we meet with, that mentions it is Aristotle, in his book concerning the world.* Pg11

[87]*The province where the Gauls arrived and intermingled with the Greeks was called Galatia. For this reason the region was named Gallo-Graecia and afterward Galatia.* Though intermixed with the Greeks, the Galamans retained their original tongue, since we are assured by St. Jerome that in his day they spoke the same language as the Treviri in Gaul.

Polybius 200–118 BC a Greek historian gives us the earliest impression of the Gauls who invaded Macedonia. [88]*Gallogracia or Galatia, an extensive country of Asia Minor, occupied by a horde of Gauls. This Asiatic colony was, in fact, but a detachment of those vast hordes which had wandered from Gaul under the conduct of Brennus, and with which that leader invaded Greece.*
When the Roman senate, satisfied with having broken the power of the Gallo-Graeci, allowed them to retain possession of the country and forsake their former wandering and marauding habits. The whole of Galation had been divided into four parts, each governed by a separate chief named tetrarch.

---

[85] The Anabasis of Alexander, Or, The History of the Wars and Conquests of Alexander the Great
Arrian Hodder and Stoughton, 1884 Footnote on page125
[86] The introduction; the ancient state of Britain. Bedforshire Essex Thomas Cox, Anthony Hall, Robert Morden 1738
[87] Commentary on Galatians, Jerome CUA Press, 2010 pg.
[88] A Classical Dictionary: Containing ... Proper Names Mentioned in Ancient Authors, and Intended to Elucidate ... Points Connected with the Geography, History, Biography, Mythology and Fine Arts of the Greeks and Romans ... an Account of Coins, Weights and Measures ... by Charles Anthon, Harper & Bros., 1841 page 543

Figure 35. 20th century photos a). Couple from Republic of Dagestan in Russia, located in the North Caucasus region b). European Americans during the great depression

89

And now it will be worth while to declare that which multitudes are altogether ignorant of. Those who inhabit the inland parts beyond Massilia*, and about the Alps, and on this side the Pyrenean mountains, are called Celts; but those that inhabit below this part called Celtica, southward to the ocean and the mountain Hyrcinus, and all as far as Scythia, are called Gauls. But the Romans call all these people generally by one and the same name, Gauls.

For stature they are tall, but of a sweaty and pale complexion, red haired, not only naturally, but they endeavour all they can to make it redder by art. pg 314

The women here are both as tall and as courageous as the men. The children, for the most part, from their very birth are grey-headed; but when they grow up to men's estate, their hair changes in colour like to their parents. Those towards the north, and bordering upon Scythia, are so exceeding fierce and cruel, that (as report goes) they eat men, like the Britains that inhabit Iris†.

They are so noted for a fierce and warlike people, that some have thought them to be those that antiently overran all Asia, and were then called Cimerians, and who are now (through length of time) with a little alteration, called Cimbrians.

Antiently they gave themselves to rapine and spoil, wasting and destroying other countries, and slighted and despised all other people. These are they that took Rome, and robbed the temple at Delphos. These brought a great part of Europe and Asia under tribute, and possessed themselves of some of the countries of those they subdued. Because of their mixture with the Grecians, they were at last called Gallo-Grecians. They often routed and destroyed many great armies of the Romans.

89 The Historical Library of Diodorus the Sicilian: In Fifteen Books. To which are Added the Fragments of Diodorus, and Those Published by H. Valesius, I. Rhodomannus, & F. Ursinus, translated by G Booth ESQ
Harvard College Library In two volumes. Vol. 1 printed by W.M Dowall 1814 pg. 314-317

[90]This practice of cannibalism is believed to have continued well into the 18th century; and those who invaded South Africa, in the age of Nelson Mandela, boasted of having barbeques of the Africans. But the language of the Greeks in general, did not change much, partly because the Grecian language was an [91]*abstraction made from a collection of dialects.* [92]*Greek was borrowed directly from the Phoenician language.*

An Ethnographic Portrait of Ancient Europe

Herodotus (5th century BC) is the first to actually create a distinctive picture of the various European peoples. He mentions eight tribes most of these have mingled and some are now extinct, so the European people today represent a more recent admixture of Jews, Romans, Africans and Asians:

[93]*Tauroi/Taurians, Agathyrsians, Neuro/Neuriansi, Androphagoi/ Androphages, Melanchlainoi/Melanchaenians, Gelonians, Budinoi/Budians and Sauromati/Samaritans. Tauroi make their living by plunder and war.*
Agathyrsians are most luxurious of men, they wear gold ornaments and live promiscuously. They resemble Thracians in other customs.
Neuroi/ Neurians were forced to quit their land altogether because of serpents and settled among the Budinoi/Budians
The Scythians consider them wizards who transform into wolves a few days a year.
Androphagoi/Androphages have the most savage manners of all human beings, and they neither acknowledge any rule of right nor observe any customary law. They are nomads and wear clothing like the scythians, but have a language of their own and are man eaters. (origin of vampires)
Budinoi are a great numerous race, and are all very blue-eyed and fair of skin:

The Gelonians are originally Hellenes, settled among the Budinoi; and in their land is built a city of wood. There are temples of Hellenic Gods in the Hellenic fashion all of wood. They use partly the Scythian language and partly the Hellenic. They do not live in the same manner as the Budinoi, for the Budinoi are natives of the soil and a nomad people who feed on fircones; but the Gelonians are tillers of the ground and feed on corn and have gardens, and resemble them not at all either in appearance or in complexion of skin. The land is all thickly overgrown with forests and trees.102-114 (The Gelonians may have been a branch of the new Romans who moved North of Italy)

---

90 The Ancient Laws of Cambria: Containing the Institutional Triads of Dyonwal Moelmud, Howel the Good... and the Hunting Laws of Wales, to which are Added the Historical Triads Or Britain. Translated from the Welsh, by William Probert. - London, William Probert, 1823 pg. 391
91 A History of Ancient Greek: From the Beginnings to Late Antiquity by Anastasios-Phoivos Christidēs, Maria Arapopoulou, Maria Chritē, Cambridge University Press, Jan 11, 2007
92 Encyclopedia Americana volume 16 Latin. 1956Pg 765
93 The Histories of Herodotus. Volumes I and II (complete) by G. C. Macaulay (Translated) MobileReference, 2010

Diodorus says that *Carthagians, were resolved to do their utmost to subdue all the cities of Sicily; but before they transported their armies, having got together out of Carthage, and other cities in Africa, many that were willing to transport themselves, they built a new city called Thernia, near the hot baths in Sicily.*

But [94]*Carthaginian domination of the seas had to be challenged. So Rome created her first ever large fleet of warships.* This began a series of three wars in 218 BC which were called Punic wars.
Punic [=Carthaginian, since Carthage was a colony of Phoenicia, whose people the Romans called Punici]
[95]*Unlike the Greek, the Latin alphabet* was not *borrowed directly from the Phoenician but through the medium of the Greek alphabet of the Doric-Chalcidian colony of lower Italy.*

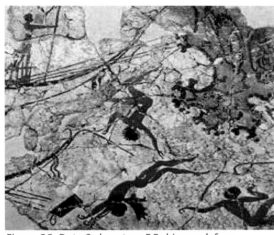

Figure 36. Date 3rd century BC shipwreck from Excavation at Akrotiri on the island of Santorini.

The Romans achieved great success in the first War to the surprise of the Carthaginians. The Carthaginians were more prepared by the second war, and won under the direction of one of the most inventive generals of all time, Hannibal.

After the First Punic War, Rome wrested Corsica and Sardinia from the Carthaginians. Hannibal moved north to capture a base in Spain, to attack the Romans unexpectedly by land. Hannibal also hoped to gather intelligence from the Gauls on developing a new route into Italy.
Polybius tells us that Hannibal first moved into Spain and the territory of the Gauls "probably in France" then rosed the Gauls against their Roman overlords. Hannibal feared the notorious betrayal of the Gauls so he disguised his men in Gaulic attire and also wigs of Gaulic hair.

Based on the advice of the Gauls, Hannibal took the best route into Italy to remain undetected; but this was also a very treacherous one. Hannibal led 50,000 foot soldiers, 9000 cavalry, and 37 war elephants over the Pyrennees and the Alps; but arrived in the plain of the Po River valley in 216 BC with only 20,000 infantry and 6,000 cavalry and the only elephant which survived was his own.
[96]*Few battles in history are more marked by ability, on the one side and crass blundering on the other, than the battle of Cannae.*
Hannibal's loss had been barely 6000 men, but he had annihilated the splendid army of eighty-seven thousand men-the flower of Rome. It had vanished as if swallowed up in an earthquake.
On his right, facing the allied cavalry, were his Numidians, 2000 strong. Of the infantry, the Spaniards and Gauls were in the center in alternate bodies. His best troops, the

[94] The World of Rome: An Introduction to Roman Culture
Peter V. Jones, Keith C. Sidwell, Cambridge University Press, Mar 6, 1997 pg. 16
[95] Encyclopedia Americana volume 16 Latin. 1956Pg 765
[96] Great Captains: A Course of Six Lectures Showing the Influence on the Art of War of the Campaigns of Alexander, Hannibal, Cæsar, Gustavus Adolphus, Frederick, and Napoleon by Theodore Ayrault Dodge Houghton Miffin, 1889 pg. 49-57

African foot, he placed on their either flank. He expected these veterans to leaven the whole lump. The foot was all in phalanxes of 1000 and 24 men each, the African foot in 16 ranks as usual, the Spaniards and Gauls in 10. Hannibal's victories were won by stratagem, or by tactical genius and skillful use of cavalry arm, not brute fighting.

Figure 37 Hannibal Fresco Capitolinec 1510

In 216 BC the Romans arrived at Cannae. The morning of the battle was unusually dark and misty, the darkness concealed all objects from view. Fifteen thousand Romans led by Quintus Fabius Maximus Cunctator were killed. When the mist and fog rose the remaining soldiers saw the massacre. Hannibal lost no more than fifteen hundred men, the greater part of whom were Gauls. His hold over northern Italy was thus established. The Carthaginians reestablished their presence on the island in 215 and maintained it until 210. But refrained from attacking the city of Rome, even after their annihilation of the Roman army. [97]Polybius explains that this was *because of the cold and nastiness, to which they had been exposed while they encamped in Gaul during the winter, and partly from the fatigue which they had suffered in their march, afterwards through the marshes, both men and horses were covered with a kind of leprous scurf; a disease, which is usually the consequence of famine and continued hardships. Book iii page 376*

In the end though the Roman cities had been defeated in two successive battles, not one single city joined the Carthaginians. Despite all of Hannibal's success *the Roman people rose with redoubled strength from every fall. The haughty Carthage, the tyrant of Spain and Afric, the sovereign mistress of commerce and the sea, bends her neck to the yoke, and the Roman* general Publius Scipio *retraced all of their advances step by step until they were compelled to surrender.* At last the Carthaginian army, was defeated at Zama. The Roman army won a decisive battle at Ilipa in 206 and forced the Carthaginians out of Spain. After his Spanish victory, Scipio determined to invade the Carthaginian homeland. Hannibal maintained his position in southern Italy until 203, when he was forced to return to Africa. (Bk iii)

The only empire left between Rome and the title for world domination was Greece; but after Greece was invaded the new citizens could not maintain power.

Figure 38 Perseus 212-166 BC was the last king of the Antigonid dynasty.

Perseus 212 – 166 BC was the last king of the Antigonid dynasty, he ruled Macedon until the Battle of Pydna in 168 BC.; subsequently Macedon fell under Roman rule.

[97]The General History of Polybius, Volume by Polybius J. Johnson; Wilkie and Robinson; J. Walker; R. Lea; J. Richardson; and J. Faulder, 1809

The Iron Legs of Italy and Axum *168 BC - 476 AD*

Figure 39. a) Head of Roman Emperor Septimius Severus (A.D. 193-211), From Ostia or the Portus. On display at the Museum of Fine Arts, Boston: b).His son Emperor Caracalla. Rome, Roman National Museum, Palazzo Massimo at the Baths bust image by Folegandros National Museum of Rome – Palazzo Massimo alle Term: Caracalla constructed The Baths of Caracalla in Rome, Italy, the second largest Ro-man public baths, between AD 212 and 216, where the legendary African hero, Hercules' naked form adorns the hall. c). Hercules worshiped as a God of perfect form Paul Stevenson at the Baths: d).Sculpture of Saint Maurice at The cathedral of Saints Catherine and Maurice in Magdeburg, Germany, next to the grave of Otto I, Holy Roman Emperor. Image by Chris 73. e). Emperor Constantius I Chorus father of Constantine the Great and founder of the Constantinian dynasty. An Original bust in Antik Sammlung Museum, Berlin Image by Marcus Cyron.

After Greece fell it [98]*became the seat of schools of philosophy and rhetoric, and later when it became a Roman Province (146 B.C.) it for a long time taught its conqueror. Architects, Drama, Philosophy, History, Poets. In this period many of the finest buildings of Athens were built. At that time the city had more than 10,000 dwellings and 100,000 free inhabitants, with at least twice as many slaves.*

27 B.C. Roman Emperor Augustus annexed the remaining regions of Greece. Romans became heavily influenced by Greek culture, Greek science, technology and mathematics. Greek-speaking communities of the Hellenized East were instrumental in the spread of early Christianity in the 2nd and 3rd centuries. Although Greece retained some of its ancient pagan religious practices until the end of the 4th century with some areas remaining pagan until well into the 10th century AD.

[99]Differential Greek and northern African migrations to Sicily are supported by genetic evidence from the Y chromosome. African Diseases like sickle cell anemia are also found among Grecian and Lebanese people in significant amounts.

While Rome raised to power a new prophet rose with it. This was no ordinary prophet, he was the son of God. Jesus was actually brought back to Egypt after his birth, so that the saying of the prophecy is fulfilled, *Out of Egypt I called my son, Mathew 2:13-15.*

This was the king of the Earth, the literal son of God riding in on a donkey *Mathew 21:5.*

---

[98] The new student's reference work a cyclopædia for teachers, students, and families, Volume 1 pg76 Chandler Belden Beach, Graeme Mercer Adam F.E. Compton & Co., 1908 By Frank Morton McMurry

[99] Cornelia Di Gaetano,1,10* Nicoletta Cerutti,1,10 Francesca Crobu,1,11 Carlo Robino,2 Serena Inturri,2 Sarah Gino,2 Simonetta Guarrera,3 Peter A Underhill,4 Roy J King,5 Valentino Romano,6 Francesco Cali,7 Mauro Gasparini,8 Giuseppe Matullo,1,3 Alfredo Salerno,9 Carlo Torre,2 and Alberto Piazza1

The word emitted from Egypt through a narrow canal in the Red Sea became flesh. This was the king that the Jews had long waited for, the miracle they desperately needed to see;

But *he came unto his own, and his own received him not.* John 1:11

They did not believe in Jesus and sought more signs and confirmations to which Jesus replied: *An evil and adulterous generation seeketh after a sign; and there shall no sign be given to it, but the sign of the prophet Jonah. For as Jonah was three days and three nights in the whale's belly; so shall the Son of man be three days and three nights in the heart of the earth.* Matthew 12: 39 & 40

The people of Nineveh idolized the fish, just like the ancient Jews did the Egyptians. Thus, like Jonah saved Nineveh, Jesus' illustrated his divine connection. By this time, the line of the priesthood had been mingled, but Jesus provided *as many as received him, with the power to become the sons of God. Which were born, not of blood, nor of the will of the flesh, nor of the will of man, but of God. John 1:12-13* The good news was that, now there was an adoption process; which allowed any believer to fuse with the likeness and image of God, by walking in his footsteps. They also took on a new name as a derivative of Christ and became Christians. From his arrival, time became measured by the period *Before Christ* to the period *After* his *Departure*, B.C. or A.D. respectively.

But for those nations which would embrace his teachings, Isaiah promised peace, civility and societal organization. T*he government shall be upon his shoulder: and his name shall be called Wonderful, Counsellor, The mighty God, The everlasting Father, The Prince of Peace.* Isaiah 9:6

The 19th chapter in the book of Acts, tells us that the message of Christianity was very disruptive to the artisans, who made their living through casting images of their Goddess Diana. Christianity's popularity meant a loss of revenue to the artisans; so Rome did not embrace this new ideology, and endeavored to persecute all Christians and Jews. In 49 AD Roman Emperor Claudius, believed that he had solved all his problems with the forced expulsion of the Jews.

The apostle Paul *found a certain Jew named Aquila, born in Pontus, lately come from Italy, with his wife Priscilla; (because that Claudius had commanded all Jews to depart from Rome) and came unto them.* Acts18:2

But in 63 AD Providence responded with a great earthquake in the Campania region where Paul and his followers had been imprisoned: a*nd at midnight Paul and Silas prayed, and sang praises unto God: and the prisoners heard them. And suddenly there was a great earthquake, so that the foundations of the prison were shaken:*

Figure 40. Stone turned victims, Pompeii. by Lancevortex.
Painting by Joseph Wright of Derby 1734

and immediately all the doors were opened, and every one's bands were loosed. Acts 16: 25

Seven years later In 70 AD the Romans returned fire, by fulfilling the [100]prophecy concerning the temple in Jerusalem and destroyed it. Then in 79 AD the eruption of Vesuvius (which had been sleeping since the time of Lot) buried Pompeii and with it paganism. Its inhabitants were also left as pillars of stone. The volcano left the emblematic pillar of fire and cloud as the decisive direction of the spirit; but Roman

[100] Luke 21:6

generals continued to work very hard to extract Christianity from Rome and to keep the country under its pagan ideology.

Tacitus, Publius/Gaius, Cornelius 56 - 117 AD said Juba reigned in Mauritania, deriving his title from the favor of Rome and three legions were stationed in Africa.

Figure 41 a) Bust of Ptolemy XII Auletes (117 BC–51 BC). Marble, 1st century BC. From Egypt. Louvre Museum Bequest of Seymour de Ricci, 1943 PD
b) Bust of Juba II, king of Mauretania (25 BC–23 CE). Marble, Roman artwork, ca. Christian Era. From Cherchell (ancient Cæsarea), Algeria. Louvre Museum Excavated by Victor Waille, 1882 image by Marie-Lan Nguyen (User:Jastrow), 2007
c) Marble bust of unknown man 70 AD in Altes Museum

[101]The insurrection of the Jews, *was soon* [102]*suppressed by the vigor of Lusius Quietus, a man of Moorish race, and considered the ablest solider in the Roman army.* He is (mentioned in the talmund) from Mauritania in northwest Africa. He was the general in 117 AD, of a great number of Africans which formed part of the Roman army.

> MOOR, n. [D. *moor*; G. *mohr*; Fr. *maure*; Gr. αμαυρος, μαυρος, dark, obscure.]
> A native of the northern coast of Africa, called by the Romans from the color of the people, *Mauritania*, the country of dark-complexioned people. The same country is now called Morocco, Tunis, Algiers, &c.

He was positioned throughout Europe and the Roman provinces and was the general to be named successor to Roman Emperor Trajan. Paul was once one of these persecutors, and may have been the single most significant propellant in the rise of the Christian theology.

Then in 193 A.D. the Severen Dynasty began with the accession of Septimus Severus from Leptis Magna in Libya. He ruled for about eighteen years until his death in 211.

[103]*He founded a personal dynasty and converted the government into a military monarchy. His reign marks a critical stage in the development of the absolute despotism that characterized the later Roman Empire.*

---

[101] The History of the Jews, from the Earliest Period Down to Modern Times, Volume 2 Henry Hart Milman Hurd and Houghton, 1864 pg. 436
[102] A Dictionary of the English Language: in Two Volumes, Volume 2 by Noah Webster, Black and Young, 1832
[103] http://www.britannica.com/EBchecked/topic/536763/Septimius-Severus

Septimus brought in his own army from Africa and determined to conquer all of Europe. He established peace among the various tribes in Britain, but concentrated heavily on his home town Leptis Magna in Libya. It eventually became the capital of the new province of Tripolitania; with new monuments a new forum and basilica, and another triumphal arc like the one he built in Italy. His son Caracalla extended Roman citizenship to their African soldiers and the two nations enjoyed great relationships. This practice of liberal citizenship was evidently the ancient character of Italy, as indicated in a letter by the Hellenistic king of Macedon, Phillip V at the end of the third century B.C.

[104]*The Romans receive into the citizen body even slaves, when they have freed them, giving them a share in the magistracies, and in such a way not only have they increased their homeland, they have also sent out colonies (SIG 543). The author says that Roman victory brought obligations, not just humiliation and transient loss. In this way the Roman concept of imperium spawned the reality of empire.* Pg. 15

This may have encouraged Phillip to free the slaves from Aristotle's town.

> [11] " The Roman arms had been carried during the reign of Augustus (B. C. 19) as far as the land of the Garamantes, the modern Fezzan, and though the Roman Emperors never attempted to establish their dominion over the country, they appear to have permanently maintained friendly relations with its rulers, which enabled their officers to make use of the oasis of the Garamantes as their point of departure from which to penetrate further into the interior. Setting out from thence, a General named Septimius Plancus 'arrived at
> [105] the land of the Ethiopians, after a march of 3 months

[106]The Aksumite (Axum) Empire, was then a formidable and important nation seated in Ethiopia, and considered one of the contending powers of the time.

[107]Three notable African church fathers formed the foundation of the Christian Church.

First: Quintus Septimius Florens Tertullianus, or Tertullian (c. 160 – c. 225 AD), was the first Christian writer of Latin Christian literature sometimes referred to as "the father of Latin Christianity"

---

[104] The World of Rome: An Introduction to Roman Culture Peter V. Jones, Keith C. Sidwell, Cambridge University Press,

[105] Ancient India as Described by Ptolemy: Being a Translation of the Chapters which Describe India and Central and Eastern Asia in the Treatise on Geography Written by Klaudios Ptolemaios, the Celebrated Astronomer : with Introduction, Commentary, Map of India According to Ptolemy, and a Very Copious Index by Ptolemy, John Watson McCrindle Thacker, Spink, & Company, 1885

[106] Ftce Social Science 6-12 Staff of Research Education Association, Cynthia Metcalf, Ph.D. Research & Education Assoc., 2010 – Education

[107] The Apologies of Justin Martyr, Tertullian, and Minutius Felix: In Defence of the Christian Religion, with the Commonitory of Vincentius Lirinensis, Concerning the Primitive Rule of Faith, Translated from Their Originals: with Notes...and a Preliminary Discourse Upon Each Author. by William Reeves W.B., 1709

Second: Cyprian, canonized as Saint Cyprian (c. 200 – September 14, 258) became the bishop of Carthage in 249. He was the head bishop of the African Council of 87 members. During this time emperor Phillip the Arabian, was the first Roman emperor to be converted.

Third: Augustine of Hippo or Saint Augustine 354 – 28 August 430, was the bishop of Algeria in West Africa. His writings are considered to have laid the foundation of Western Philosophy. His most important contributions, "the City of God" and "Confessions", are still referred to today.

Armenia and Ethiopia traditionally shared some bond. This is detected in the development of the Armenian writing systems which many scholars believe was based on Ethiopia's model.

John of Ephesus (507- 586 AD) [108]says that the reigning king, Abgar the Black or Abgarus V of Edessa, (4 BC– 50AD) was converted to Christianity by Thaddeus, one of the Seventy-two Disciples.

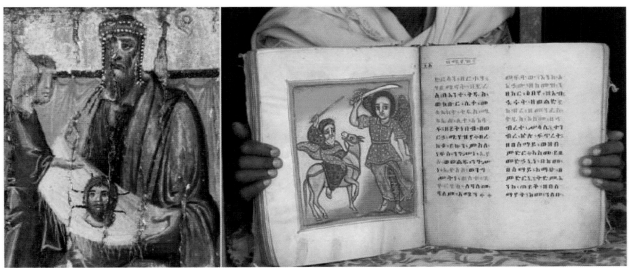

Figure 42 a) King Abgar the black of Armenia holding a picture of Jesus
b) Ethiopian Manuscript from the treasury of the Church of Narga Selassie, Dek Island, Ethiopia. by A. Davey/ Elitre

The Ethiopian kingdom was mentioned as the first to receive the gospel.

26. And the angel of the Lord spake unto Philip, saying, Arise, and go toward the south
unto the way that goeth down from Jerusalem unto Gaza, which is desert.
27 And he arose and went: and, behold, a man of Ethiopia, an eunuch of great authority under Candace
queen of the Ethiopians, who had the charge of all her treasure, and had come to Jerusalem for to worship,
28 Was returning, and sitting in his chariot read Esaias the prophet.
29 Then the Spirit said unto Philip, Go near, and join thyself to this chariot.
30 And Philip ran thither to him, and heard him read the prophet Esaias, and said, Understandest thou what thou readest?
31 And he said, how can I, except some man should guide me? And he desired Philip that he would come up and sit with him.

---

[108] Ancient Syriac Documents Relative to the Earliest Establishment of Christianity in Edessa and the Neighbouring Countries: From the Year After Our Lord's Ascension to the Beginning of the Fourth Century William Cureton, William Wright. Williams and Norgate, 1864 Now in the British Museum.

32 The place of the scripture which he read was this, He was led as a sheep to the slaughter; and like a lamb dumb before his hearer, so opened he not his mouth:

33 In his humiliation his judgment was taken away: and who shall declare his generation? for his life is taken from the earth.

34 And the eunuch answered Philip, and said, I pray thee, of whom speaketh the prophet this, of himself, or of some other man?

35 Then Philip opened his mouth, and began at the same scripture, and preached unto him Jesus.

36 And as they went on their way, they came unto a certain water: and the eunuch said, See, here is water; what doth hinder me to be baptized?

37 And Philip said, If thou believest with all thine heart, thou mayest. And he answered and said, I believe that Jesus Christ is the Son of God.

38 And he commanded the chariot to stand still: and they went down both into the water, both Philip and the eunuch; and he baptized him.

39 And when they were come up out of the water, the Spirit of the Lord caught away Philip, that the eunuch saw him no more: and he went on his way rejoicing. Acts 8: 26-39

This acceptance of Christianity led to the production of ecclesiastical documents and royal chronicles.

The gospel of a resurrected savior seemed to align perfectly with African theology of ancestor worship. From then on the Eunuchs of the African council became the light bearers with a mission to illuminate the world. Ethiopia was then a bridge between sub-Saharan Africa and the Mediterranean and secured its position as the main channel of trade and cultural contact between the Roman Empire and the Indian Ocean. Meanwhile the barbarians in the North began to push further and further South into Italy; while Roman forces moved north to develop these regions.

One Historian says that [109]*the Latin language gradually encroached upon, and in some measure superseded, that of the country. All genuine nationality was extinguished, and the very name of *Helvetia* (region of Germany or Switzerland) *disappeared.*

Admission to the rights of Roman citizenship, which under Caracalla, became easier than ever, had the effect of introducing Roman citizens into all situations hitherto filled by natives. Thus the latter came at length to be governed by functionaries, who acted upon wholly distinct interests from theirs; Woe to the land, exclaims an eloquent Swiss writer (Bulinger), on whose judgment-seats the stranger sits-at whose gates the stranger watches! Woe to the land divided against itself, and relying on foreigners! Woe to the people which gathers gold, but knows the use of steel no longer!

Christianity began to spread and the original announcement of the new faith has been ascribed by legends to a certain Beatus, so early as the first century; in the third century, to a Lucius Rhaetia: at the close of the fourth century to the so-called Theban Legion.

Because of this, Rome was able to summon Legions of soldiers in her defense, to contain invasions by the northern tribes. This legion was led by Saint Maurice, who when he arrived found that the residents

---

[109]History of Switzerland, from B.C. 110, to A.D. 1830 By Dionysius Lardner 1832 page 29 * Original name of Southern Germany or Switzerland.

were converted Christians and refused to harm them. The town of St. Moritz/ad sanctum Mauricium in Switzerland was named after him. West Africans from Mauritania were referred to as *"Moors"*. The name Maurice may have simply stood for black men; so all that remains of the legend is a face and this corresponding description.

This legion from Egypt must have made a lasting impression because pilgrims continued to travel to Saint Mauritius for centuries.

Then at the end of the third century a Libyan bishop named Arius developed a doctrine later termed as [110]Arianism. A council of bishops convened to denounce this theology which contested the divinity of Christ. The Nicene Creed, was adopted as a formal definition of Christianity in opposition to Arian theology.

> **11. On the meeting of the 318 Orthodox at Nice, and their Council, formed to promote the purity of the faith.**
>
> **18. Relates the meeting of the 318 bishops (likan papasat), at which, (c. 19 and 20) Damatius, the Roman bishop, stood up, and said he had found a book on the division of the world in the church of Sophia. In this volume it was recorded, that the earth was divided between the king of Rome and the king of Ethiopia The work concludes with observations on the kings of Romia and Ethiopia, between whom the world is divided in this manner : " All the globe, north of Jerusalem, belongs to the former, and south of it to the latter."**
>
> **Such is the outline of the Kebir Neguste, the glory of the Kings, usually called the Book, or Chronicle of Axum. It be a translation of a treatise found in the church of St Sophia by Damatius, bishop of Romia (perhaps Constantinople, and read at** [111] **the council of Nice !**

If we consider the chronicles of the Axumite Empire, as well as the reference from the book of Acts, then Rome and Axum stood together as the legs of our statue, contemplating how to govern the world.

[112]A few years later in 327AD Constantine Emperor of Rome, dreamt of victory in an impending battle, if he fought under the symbol of the cross. The Romans believed that this was a sign to embrace Christianity as a national religion, to retain their slipping control over the North. They later recognized the Christian church as a legal body and united the Christians and pagans; but this meant compromise. The pagan Sunday was substituted for the Sabbath and idols were renamed to match Christian deities and saints. Thus Daniel's prophecy of *changing time (or days) and Laws* was fulfilled. Daniel 7:25

This merger brought the persecution of Christians to an end and solidified Rome and eventually the Vatican as a world power, but not in the way they imagined.

---

[110] Arian doctrine was a theological perspective of Arius a Libyan Priest in Alexandria, Egypt, of the church of Baucalis; which Arius posed in his letter to Eusebius of Nicomedia denies that the Son is of one essence, nature, or consubstantial (homoousios) with the Father, thus unlike Him, and unequal in dignity. (250-336 AD)

[111] Travels to Discover the Source of the Nile, in the Years 1768, Volume 3 - Page 409-417 James Bruce 1813

[112] The Cambridge Ancient History: Volume 12, The Crisis of Empire, AD 193-337
edited by Alan Bowman, Averil Cameron, Peter Garnsey P6 92 Constantine's dream

Figure 43 14th century: Miniature 32 from the Constantine Manasses Chronicle, Roman emperors Arcadius, Honorius and Theodosius I.

Theodosius I (379-395 AD) was the last emperor to rule over both the eastern and the western halves of the Roman Empire, after battling Eugenius, his Arian contender. The controversy of the interpretation of the doctrine and the schism brought about by Arius, continued; and the [113]*heresy of those who ventured upon enumerating the natures and substances and Godheads and Gods in the holy and consubstantial trinity. The epostacy founded by Conon and Eugenius, the heads of the heresy of a multitude of Gods, was in fact contrary to the canons and constitutions of the church, nevertheless, whoever came in their way, whether young or old, unlearned or wise and so to speak, they made them all bishops and sent them in all directions and to all countries, and so gathered congregations in Rome and Corinth and Athens and Africa, and led simple minded people astray after them.*

Eugenius was later captured and executed, and Theodosius enforced Nicene Christianity as the official state religion of the Roman Empire. After his death, the Empire was divided under his sons Arcadius in the Eastern portion and his eight year old son Honorius in the West.

[114]

> **Now while Honorius was holding the imperial power in the West, barbarians took possession of his land; and I shall tell who they were and in what manner they did so. There were many Gothic nations in earlier times, just as also at the present, but the greatest and most important of all are the Goths, Vandals, Visigoths, and Gepaedes. In ancient times, however, they were named Sauromatae and Melanchlaeni;[1] and there were some too who called these nations Getic. All these, while they are distinguished from one another by their names, as has been said, do not differ in anything else at all. For they all have white bodies and fair hair, and are tall and handsome to look upon, and they use the same laws and practise a common religion. For they are all of the Arian faith, and have one language called Gothic; and, as it seems to me, they all came originally from one tribe, and were distinguished later by the names of those who led each group.**

From the 5th century churches and monasteries were being built and the Roman Catholic Church started to form. Hundreds of statues of the Virgin Mary called, Black Madonna can be found in churches throughout Europe including Russia and Germany, and they portray a black Mary and Jesus. The color

---

[113] The third part of the ecclesiastical history of John bishop of Ephesus, (507- 586 AD) tr. by R.P. Smith by Johannes (bp. of Ephesus.) 1860 52-54
[114] Procopius 500-562AD: History of the wars, Books III and IV (Vandalic War) Translated by, Harvard University Press, 1916 pg 9-11

cannot be attributed to the medium because many are painted on wood, and stone and just a few are dark because of a bronze base. Some have claimed that these are remnants of the pagan worship of Isis; which may have been transported there by the Gelonian people, mentioned by Herodotus.

But we may assume that many of these statues were part of the churches built by the Romans, because: [115]

> **16.** It is a well-known fact that the peoples of Germany have no cities, and that they do not even allow buildings to be erected close together.[4] They live scattered about, wherever a spring, or a meadow, or a wood has attracted them. Their villages are not arranged in the Roman fashion, with the buildings connected and joined together, but every person surrounds his dwelling with an open space, either as a precaution against the disasters **Lack of cities** of fire, or because they do not know how to build. **and towns** They make no use of stone or brick, but employ wood for all purposes. Their buildings are mere rude masses, without ornament or attractiveness, although occasionally they are stained in part with a kind of clay which is so clear and bright that it resembles painting, or a colored design. . . .
>
> 30   THE EARLY GERMANS

Before the Romans, and apart from the Gelonians, there were no buildings, churches or artisans. There are virtually no artifacts before this era which demarcate a Northern European civilization; so these images tell us more about the history of Europe and the presence of a population, which has disappeared.

Figure 44. a) One of the earliest images of Mary and Jesus (2nd Century) in the Catacomb of Priscilla in Rome.
b) 11th or 12th Century Theotokos of Vladimir, also known as Our Lady of Vladimir or Virgin of Vladimir one of the most venerated Russian icons. The icon is displayed in the Tretyakov Gallery, Moscow. (Notice the hands are much darker, looks like the paint was washed out from the faces.)

[116][117]The earliest Frescos have been attributed to the Apostle Luke. Those found in Roman catacombs and monasteries all over Europe, indicate a dark African Mary and Jesus. Some of the earliest sculptures of the Black Virgin have been attributed to the Bishop Eusebius of Vercelli, during the reign of

---

[115] The source book of mediæval history: documents illustrative of European life and institutions from the German invasion to the Renaissance by Frederic Austin 1907 pages 29-31
[116] A Handbook for Travellers in Northern Italy &c Murray, 1863 pg508
[117] The gentleman's guide in his tour through Italy- Thomas Martyn, 1791 pg123

Constantine and the beginning of the Roman Catholic Church. The bishop is said to have brought back, black painted cedar sculptures from the Middle Eastern Region.

Virgin Mary Statues throughout Europe

Figure 45 a). Church of St. Kastulus Moosburg an der Isar Oberbayern by Mattana
b).Capuchin-church, Bahnhofstraße:Klagenfurt, Austria by Mefusbren69
c).Kapelle Maria im Schnee (Wuppertal-Beyenburg)by Velopilger
d).Statue de la Vierge noire (XII siècle); Moulins Cathédrale by Sergey Prokopenko
e).Eisenstadt, Mountain Church Vienna by Pe-Jo
f).13th century altar in Positano on the Amalfi Coast Italy. Vincent de Paul Basilica in Bydgoszcz PD

These images are reminiscent of the founders of the Christian mission into Europe and provide a glimpse into the developing perceptions of the race which taught them. In reverse order the European colonists of the New World brought the gospel to Native Americans and then African slaves and their image of Jesus was like their own.

Figure 46 1-3 Hurculerum Frescos of Roman men with captured women 4 [oralia 35cC] Black Priest Holding Sistrun and Black Musicians Backgrounds of Early Christianity by Everett Ferguson Wm. B. Eerdmans Publishing, 2003 5. A porphyry sculpture of Four Tetrarchs a group of Roman emperors that governed the Roman Empire dating from around 300 AD.

The attempt to remove paint and add curls to the hair is obvious on some of these; but the most ancient sources from Herodotus more the 2400 years ago to Romans like Diodorus the Sicilian 2050 years ago, as recent as Tacitus and Pliny in the first century, John of Ephesus and Procobius as late as the 6th century, then Arabians just about 1000 years ago, make it quite evident that the idea we have come to formalize as a European nature is a very recent one. *Suddenly* we speak of German engineering and European genius, concepts which are just a few centuries removed from the descriptions of ferocity, and barbaric-heathenism. In their own words, all of the historians saw the northerners as very different from themselves, with unusually long, straight hair, and white skin

Figure 48 a) Image of a Northern woman as seen by the Romans

Italy before her invasion by the Northern tribes, was the type of integrated civilization of Africans and Europeans we consider Latinos. These Latinos were more like the colored people of South Africa, because they were connected to a steady influx of Africans throughout their history; but we can see a very clear reversal of colonialism as it relates to the building of Europe, by "Africans." The unfathomable truth is, African civilizations predate any civilization in Europe, and endured in a position of instructor for a very long time; but we have been educated to think of Africans beneath all the other people of the world. Racism continues in America because it is literally part of the curriculum.

Source — C. Cornelius Tacitus, *De Origine, Situ, Moribus, ac Populis Germanorum* [known commonly as the "Germania"], Chaps. 4–24 *passim*. Adapted from translation by Alfred J. Church and William J. Brodribb (London, 1868), pp. 1–16. Text in numerous editions, as that of William F. Allen (Boston, 1882) and that of Henry Furneau (Oxford, 1894).

4. For my own part, I agree with those who think that the tribes of Germany are free from all trace of intermarriage with **Physical characteristics** foreign nations, and that they appear as a distinct, unmixed race, like none but themselves. Hence it is that the same physical features are to be observed throughout so vast a population. All have fierce blue eyes, reddish hair, and huge bodies fit only for sudden exertion. They are not very able to endure labor that is exhausting. Heat and thirst they cannot withstand at all, though to cold and hunger their climate and soil have hardened them.

6. Iron is not plentiful among them, as may be inferred from the nature of their weapons.[1] Only a few make use of swords or long lances. Ordinarily they carry a spear (which they call a *framea*), with a short and narrow head, but so sharp and easy to handle that the same weapon serves, according to circumstances, for close or distant conflict. As for the horse-soldier, he is satisfied with a shield and a spear. The foot-soldiers also scatter

[1] In reality iron ore was abundant in the Germans' territory, but it was not until long after the time of Tacitus that much use began to be made of it. By the fifth century iron swords were common.

118

Africa developed its own iron industry some 5,000 years ago, according to a formidable new scientific work from UNESCO Publishing that challenges a lot of conventional thinking on the subject.
(These were the First Blacksmiths) United Nations Educational Scientific and Cultural Organization.

---

118 The source book of mediæval history: documents illustrative of European life and institutions from the German invasion to the Renaissance by Frederic Austin 1908 pages 22-25 & 44-46

[119]*Meanwhile the Roman power sunk lower and lower. Not misused people only, but many men of rank and power, encouraged foreign in order to get rid of domestic enemies. Under the perpetual minority of the imbecile Arcadias and Honorius, the empire, already more than once dissevered, became permanently parted into Eastern and Western.*

Precisely at this epoch of exhaustion, more numerous swarms of semi-barbarous nomad nations set themselves in motion than at any former period; the roughest and remotest of which drove the others forwards on the now defenseless frontiers of the empire.

While from the east the Goths fell upon Italy, while the Vandals and Suevi attacked Spain, the Burgundians (also a race of Vandal origin) marched on the Upper ....

The Burgundians fixed their residence on both sides of the Jura, on the lake of Geneva...They adopted Christianity on their reception as Roman allies-a title which, by this time, had completely changed its import; and instead of future subjugation, augured future mastery. They combined with large and vigorous outward proportions a character less rude than some other northern nations. In the quality of peaceable guests and new allies of the empire, they spared the still remaining towns and other Roman monuments, and permitted the former owners to retain their established laws and customs; appropriating, however, to themselves a third of the slaves, two thirds of the cultivated lands, and one half of the forests, gardens, and farm buildings.

Eastward of that stream, and over great part of Germany, the land was overrun by the Alemanni, (Germans) whose inroads on the empire may be dated somewhat later than those of the Burgundians. (A.D 450)These new comers, embittered towards whatever bore the name of Roman, destroyed the still remaining fragments of fortresses and cities, which, in common with all German tribes, they utterly detested. They did not treat the inhabitants with cruelty, but reduced them to a state of complete servitude. All Roman landed property they seized without exception, and only allowed the tenants to remain there in the situation of bondmen, and on the condition of paying them dues. This new barbarian torrent overwhelmed the public monuments and symbols of Christianity. Whatever yet remained of the old culture disappeared, or at all events concealed itself.

Now we see the images of Saint Maurice and the Black figures of Christianity, whitened or vandalized.

---

[119] History of Switzerland, from B.C. 110, to A.D. 1830 By Dionysius Lardner 1832 page 29-31
A similar account is rendered in The source book of medieval history: documents illustrative of European life and institutions from the German invasion to the Renaissance by Frederic Austin 1907

Figure 49 Maarten van Heemskerck (1498–1574 Triumphzug des Bacchus 1536-1537

Lardner continues to show how heathenism slowly encroached into all of the region.

The common people in town and country were drawn away from honest labor to idleness, lewdness, and warlike undertakings,-and reckless and abandoned habits thus prevailed everywhere."

The changing population left traces of their overwhelming influence on the classical Latin. The dialect transitioned into a less polished form known as *Vulgar Latin*, which is represented in St. Jerome's translation of the Bible the Vulgate, but the Latin language was eventually completely erased and replaced with Italian.

[120] *The Romans were suffering almost greater miseries from the inroads of an abominable people, who, from their long hair, are called Avars. Their first appearance in the Roman territories was in the days of King Justinian.*
Justinian I bought peace with gold and other gifts, *but when he died his successor refused and threated to fight them. Still prophesying to be friends, they sent ambassadors to Justin, and cunningly asked him, in the name of their king, to send artificers and masons to build a palace and a bath;* and when the masons were finished the vandals forced them to build a bridge over the Danube River.

Procopius (500- 562 AD) from the Middle East, is one of our earliest historians on this account, and the last of ancient historians. He tells us that,
[121]*The Vandals led by their king Genseric crossed into Africa in 429AD.*
They invaded North Africa with an army of 80,000 and ruled there for 26years, until they were driven away by the Moors. He also says that in his time: *the Moors of that place held also the land to the west of Aurasium, a tract both extensive and fertile. And beyond these dwelt other nations of the Moors, who were ruled by Oratais, who had come as an ally to Solomon and the*

---

[120] The third part of the ecclesiastical history of John bishop of Ephesus, tr. by R.P. Smith by Johannes (bp. of Ephesus.) 1860 428-430
[121] Procopius: History of the wars, Books III and IV (Vandalic War) Translated by, Harvard University Press, 1916 321-323

Romans. And I have heard this man say that beyond the country which he ruled there was no habitation of men, but desert land extending to a great distance and beyond that there are men, not black-skinned like the Moors, but very white in body and fair-haired. 321-323

Leo Africanus gives us this very same description almost one thousand years later. He accounts for the whites in Tunisia as Goths or vandals who invaded in the time of Saint Augustine of Hippo and apparently remained in North Africa.

[122]*Procopius and other geographers speak of it as Aurasion or Mons Aurasim; but these hardly include the entire district now known as the Aures Mountains...eastwards towards the Tunisian Frontier.*

[123]*By the first decade of the sixth century AD the vandals were beginning to be absorbed into the mass of the Afro-Latin population. In this respect the religious and social history of North Africa resembles that of Burgundy, Spain and Italy at this period.*

This final invasion of Rome was followed by the subsequent destruction of the nation through plagues and famines. By the mid-sixth century, the plague which was named after the Emperor Justinian who contracted the disease seemed to follow the route of the vandals into Rome and North Africa. Scholars believe that the plague killed up to 5,000 people per day in Constantinople at the peak of the pandemic. It ultimately killed perhaps 40% of the city's inhabitants. The initial plague went on to destroy up to a quarter of the eastern Mediterranean population. Procopius tells us that Rome was sparsely populated.
[124]

the barbarians, finding that they had no hostile force to encounter them, became the most cruel of all men. For they destroyed all the cities which they captured, especially those south of the Ionian Gulf, so completely that nothing has been left to my time to know them by, unless, indeed, it might be one tower or one gate or some such thing which chanced to remain. And they killed all the people, as many as came in their way, both old and young alike, sparing neither women nor children. Wherefore even up to the present time Italy is sparsely populated. They also gathered as plunder all the money out of all Europe, and, most important of all, they left in Rome nothing whatever of public or

---

[122] 1876 Report by the British Association for the Advancement of Science
[123] The Cambridge History of Africa, Volume 2 J. D. Fage, Roland Anthony Oliver, Cambridge University Press, 1978 pg. 483
[124] Procopius: History of the wars, Books III and IV (Vandalic War) Translated by, Harvard University Press, 1916 pg9-11

West African Toes *500 – 1700 AD*

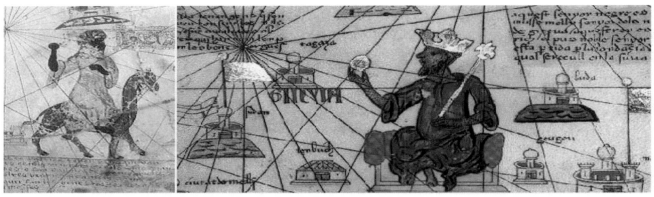

Figure 50 a) Almoravid general Abu Bakr ibn Umar on a camel, portolan chart of Mecia Viladestes. 1413
Bibliothèque nationale de France
B)Musa holding a gold nugget on the Catalan Atlas 1375.

After the vandals invaded Italy, they were unable to continue leading the country; so the Roman Empire collapsed. The whole world seemed to stand on one leg, as the Ethiopian empire grew larger and larger and extended to the farthest regions of India, Sri Lanka, the gold mines of Great Zimbabwe and West African kingdoms.

By the end of the 7th century A.D. the prophet Mohamed gave birth to the ideology of Islam. His disciples spread into Africa and begun to threaten the decree to spread the Christian gospel throughout the world. The Axum Empire struggled under the growing influence of Muslims, who sought refuge there.

Then [125]*In 747 earthquake damage forced the transfer of the center of the Islamic caliphate from Syria to Iraq and by 750 Amman's prosperity declined* and many Arabians begun moving west.

[126]*after the Mahumetans got the dominion of Egypt the nobility of Egypt retired themselves into the inland.*

[127]Diodorus our trusted historian, calculated only three million people living in Egypt in his time, from an estimated seven million in ancient times. Then in the 19th century John Murray visited Egypt and estimated about two and a half million citizens; more than eighty percent were then Arabians, with a population of only 150,000 Coptic Christians who were then considered descendants from the ancients, but with many having mixed with the Arabians.

This westward movement of Egyptians brought a wave of Empire builders into Western Africa and eventually Western Europe. But these too, were later influenced by the Muslim doctrine which grew into an African stampede heading for Europe. In 711 AD, the moors from North and West Africa captured Spain and reigned there for over 500 years.

---

[125] The Grove Encyclopedia of Islamic Art and Architecture, Volume 3 Jonathan M. Bloom, Sheila Blair
Oxford University Press, 2009 – Art
[126] The History and Description of Africa: And of the Notable Things Therein Contained (Google eBook)
Leo (Africanus), Robert Brown, John Pory Hakluyt Society, 1896 pg. 859
[127] An Account of the manners and customs of the modern Egyptians, Edward William Lane
John Murray, 1860. Pg. 22-24

[128]Spain quickly became the most prominent European nation and experienced its greatest periods of prosperity. Early attempts to regain European territory from the invading Moors, was fought in the Battle of Roncesvalles at the end of the 8th century, between the Northern army and the Moors. Modern accounts of African history would lead us to believe that Arabian tribes were responsible for this advance into Spain; but many historians tell us that the Arabian immigrants were still living in tents and had not been established by this time. Besides their accounts, we can tell from the fall of Egypt and the rise of the western regions that the pattern of development came from the already advanced East Africans.

Roland, a bold warrior of the Frankish court died in this battle; but left us a firsthand account, recorded in *the Song of Roland*. It is the **oldest** surviving major work of French literature; with nine extant manuscripts in the Old French dialect.

Figure 51 The Saracen/Moorish Army outside Paris, 730-32 AD, by Julius Schnorr von Carolsfeld, painted 1822-27

[129]*Who holds Alferne, Kartagene, Garmalie,*
And Ethiope, a cursed land indeed;
The blackamoors from there are in his keep,
Broad in the nose they are and flat in the ear,
Fifty thousand and more in company.
These canter forth with arrogance and heat,
Then they cry out the pagans' rallying-cheer;
And Rollant says: "Martyrdom we'll receive;
When Rollant sees those misbegotten men,
Who are more-black than ink is on the pen
With no part white, only their teeth except,
Then says that count: I know now very well
That here to die we're bound, as I can tell.
Strike on, the Franks! For so I recommend."
Says Oliver: "Who holds back, is condemned!"
Upon those words, the Franks to strike
again. cxlv
[130]*Blackamoor, moor defined as a Negro or*
Black person

The Franks and all of the new Christians in Europe were now the self-appointed defenders of the faith. The division was now more obviously than at any time in history, securely one of ideology. This was not a war of race, but a war of faith. Whereas war was a means of expanding an empire or a means of survival, it was now a war of ideology; with the three branches which stemmed from the Torah, Christianity, Islam and Judaism now competing for expansion. With the exclusion of the Jews, who did not care so much to share their faith.

---

[128] The Jews and Moors in Spain by Joseph Krauskopf M. Berkowitz & Company, 1886. This is the best account of the history of Spain and the invasion from the records of Arabians and the comprehensive research of this author. P228
[129] The Song of Roland: Done Into English, in the Original Measure Dutton, 1920 Pg. 63
[130] A Dictionary of the English Language: Compiled for the Use of Common Schools in the United States Noah Webster George Goodwin, 1817

Figure 52 Africa and trading Nations

The Moors in Africa who remained faithful to the Christian faith, moved into Europe and aided in the battles against their Muslim brothers in Spain and Africa.

Henry Coppée (although rife with racial bigotry) described the final battle between the Islamic and Christian ideologies. This is the prevailing theme of David against Goliath. In this account, an uneven battle between the Christian King and the Muslims ended in the unexpected defeat of the Almoravid Muslims.

> The array of the Moslem chief was of unusual splendor. The imperial tent, which was pitched upon an eminence commanding the entire field, was of three-The fortified tent of Mohammed An-Nassir. ply crimson velvet (*terciopelo, carmesí con flecos de oro*) flecked with gold; and its purple fringes were ornamented with rows of pearls. To guard it there were towards the enemy rows of iron chains, and a line of three thousand camels; in front of which, with lances planted upright in the sand, was a living wall of ten thousand hideous negroes, in African costumes. [131]

Various kings rose up in Africa, to seize control of the north western empire. The Abasside Dynasty ruled North Africa from 974 AD well into the 11th century. In West Africa the Aghlasbite dynasty ruled for 100 years from 800 to 920. The Fatimid's besieged Fez in 920 AD followed by the Omayyad's in 973. Ghana flourished from about 300 to 1000 AD. Then the Almoravids founded by Yusuf IBN Tashfin, conquered the Ghanaian Empire and seized Fez in 1063, Medilla and Tangies in 1084 and in 1086 they met with the army of Alfonso VI (of Spain) and defeated the Christians. Yusuf ibn Tashfin founded the city of Marrakech and led the Muslim forces in the Battle of Zallaqa/Sagrajas

[132]*By the year 1095 the whole of Moorish Spain was in the hands of the new invaders, forming an integral part of a vast empire whose center of gravity was in Morocco, and whose southern limit was in Senegal.*

In 1248 The Merinites took over Fez and by 1269, Morocco. By the 13th Century, the Malian Empire of West Africa founded by Sundiata Keita, became renowned for the wealth of its rulers, especially Mansa Musa I, the wealthiest man alive then and in the ranks of all time. It was his predecessors who embarked on the expedition, west of the Atlantic. Which could also account for the Africans encountered by Europeans in the New World.

As early as the 12th century, Timbuktu in Mali, was the world renowned center of wealth and Islamic scholarship. Scholars from as far away as Persia, Cairo and Baghdad took the treacherous journey for months across the sands of the Sahara to study there. [133]At its peak, over 25,000 students attended the University of Timbuktu. The Ahmed Baba Research Center houses the largest collection of sacred manuscripts that date back over some 600 years. Some scholars estimate that there are over 700,000 manuscripts housed throughout private collections in Timbuktu.

Joannes Leo Africanus, 1494 - 1554

Figure 53 Leo Africanus 1519 by sebastiano del piombo

Then in the 16th century, Leo Africanus, arrived in Africa during the reign of Hajj Mohammed Ben Abu Bakr Askia; whom he calls, Ischia or Abuacre Izchia. This king rose against Abu Bakr Dau in 1488 and captured Timbuktu and most of West Africa and governed almost all the provinces as one until 1537.

---

[131] History of the conquest of Spain by the Arab-Moors: With a sketch of the civilization which they achieved, and imparted to Europe, Volume 2 Henry Coppée, Little, Brown, 1881

[132] The Rise of the Spanish Empire in the Old World and in the New, Volume 1 by Roger Bigelow Merriman Macmillan, 1918 page 14-23

[133] Reclaiming the Ancient Manuscripts of Timbuktu by Chris Rainier for National Geographic News May 27, 2003

Figure 54. Rudolf Ernst later exhibiting as Rodolphe Ernst was an Austrian-born orientalist painter in Paris (Vienna, 14 February 1854 - Fontenay-aux-Roses, 1932) more under end notes of African Portraits.

Leo Africanus is best known for his book Descrittione dell'Africa (Description of Africa) which describes the geography of North Africa. This inadvertently laid the ground work for colonial invasions.

He described the entire continent as he saw it in the 16th century.

Alguechet was a very wealthy nation West of Egypt.

Of the region of Alguechet.

ALguechet also being a region of the Libyan desert, is from Egypt an hundred and twenty miles distant. Here are three castles and many villages abounding with dates. The inhabitants are black, vile, and couetous people, and yet exceeding rich : for they dwell in the mid way betweene Egypt and Gaoga. They haue a gouernour of their owne, notwithstanding they pay tribute vnto the next Arabians.[67]

Here endeth the sixth booke.

[134]Leo describes the North African landscape.

Of the region of Tesebit.

THe region of Tesebit being situate vpon the Numidian desert, two hundred and fiftie miles eastward of Segelmesse, and an hundred miles from mount Atlas, hath fower castles within the precincts thereof, and many villages also, which stand vpon the confines of Lybia, neer vnto the high way that leadeth from Fez and Telensin to the kingdome of Agadez and to the land of Negros. The inhabitants are not very rich, for all their wealth consisteth in dates, and some small quantitie of corne. The men of this place are black, but the women are somewhat fairer, and yet they are of a swart and browne hue.[38]

Numidians (of todays Algeria) *of Guargala* (he says) *are rich, all of a black color, and have black slaves.* I connected the etymology of Numidian to the ancient Midians during the priesthood of Moses. Remember that Nu-midia like New England, was a colony planted by the Pheonicians from the wealthy nation of Midia or the Persian Medea. (page 54) Nu, is very similar from the Latin root Novi which may be consistent with the Punic.

---

[134] The History and Description of Africa: And of the Notable Things Therein Contained by Leo (Africanus), Robert Brown, John Pory Hakluyt Society, 1896 pg. 776

THis ancient citie built by the Romaines vpon the Mediterran sea, was fortified with most high and stately walles, and with a strong castle.[74] It hath continually been so molested by the Arabians,

The inhabitants of the foresaide plaine are blacke people, being all of them either fishers, or husbandmen.

Of the village of Guaden.

THis village situate vpon the Numidian desert neere unto Libya, And these people also are blacke of colour.[13]

Of the citie of Guargala.

His ancient citie founded by the Numidians, and enuironed with strong wals vpon the Numidian desert, is built very sumptuously, and aboundeth exceedingly with dates. It hath some castles and a great number of villages belonging thereunto. The inhabitants are rich, bicause they are neere vnto the kingdome of Agadez. Heere are diuers merchants of Tunis and Constantina, which transport wares of Barbarie vnto the lande of Negros. And bicause flesh and corne is very scarce with them, they liue vpon the flesh of Ostriches and camels. They are all of a blacke colour, and haue blacke slaues, and are people of a courteous and liberall disposition, and most friendly and bountifull vnto strangers. A gouernour they haue whom they reuerence as if he were a king : which gouernour hath about two thousand horsemen alwaies attending vpon him, and collecteth almost fifteene thousand ducates for yeerely reuenue.[42]

Leo says of the king of Mali, that:

He so deadly hateth all Iewes, that he will not admit any into his citie : and whatsoeuer Barbarie merchants he vnderstandeth haue any dealings with the Iewes, he presently causeth their goods to be confiscate. Here are great store of doctors, iudges, priests, and other learned men, that are bountifully maintained at the kings cost and charges. And hither are brought diuers manuscripts or written bookes out of Barbarie, which are sold for more money than any other merchandize.[10]

In this kingdome there is a large and ample village containing to the number of sixe thousand or mo families, and called Melli, whereof the whole kingdome is so named. And here the king hath his place of residence. The region it selfe yeeldeth great abundance of corne, flesh, and cotton. Heere are many artificers and merchants in all places: and yet the king honourably entertaineth all strangers. The inhabitants are rich, and haue plentie of wares. Heere are great store of temples, priests, and professours, which professours read their lectures onely in the temples, bicause they haue no colleges at all. The people of this region excell all other Negros in witte, ciuilitie, and industry; and were the first that embraced the law of Mahumet, at the same time when the vncle of *Ioseph* the king of Maroco was their prince, and the gouernment remained for a while vnto his posterity: at length *Izchia* subdued the prince of this region, and made him his tributarie, and so oppressed him with greeuous exactions, that he was scarce able to maintaine his family.[6]

Then a little over a century later we are told that

[135]*The King of Benin can in a single day make 20,000 men ready for war, and, if need be, 180,000, and because of this he has great influence among all the surrounding peoples. . . . His authority stretches over many cities, towns and villages. There is no King thereabouts who, in the possession of so many beautiful cities and towns, is his equal.*

[136]The invasion of Sudan, began from Marrakech on October 16, 1590, when Al-Mansur, the Shariff of Morocco, invaded the Songhai Empire to capture the source of their gold. Mulai Ahmad al-Mansur also known as al-Dhahabi (the golden one) was the ruler of Morocco from 1578 -1603. Then drought was followed by pestilence in 1618.

---

[135] —Olfert Dapper, Nauwkeurige Beschrijvinge der Afrikaansche Gewesten (Description of Africa), **1668**
[136] Timbucto the Mysteries. Felix dubouis 1897 timbucto the mysteries

[137]The authors of the following portrait of Morocco, begun their expedition just two years after the death of Moulay Ismaïl Ibn or Mulley Ismael, in 1729. Mulley ruled for 55 years from 1672–1727.

Without the town-wall and parted by a road, is the Negro-Town, which is very near as large as the city, but the houses are only of thatch. These people are mostly horse-soldiers, and ready to be sent on any immediate service. The palaces, were built entirely by Muley Ismael, and stand upon more ground than the city, and indeed are rather a city than a palace. These palaces are divided into many distinct squares, and different apartments; some inhabited by the kings wives, his concubines, his tradesmen, and his guards. These different quarters of the palace, have each their proper officers to guard them and are distinct as if they were entirely separate.

Figure 55 Moulay Abd-er-Rahman, Sultan of Morocco, leaving his palace in Meknes, surrounded by the Elite Black Guards and his principal officers. Painting from 1845

The Negro eunuchs guarding the women's apartments. One may as properly call the tower of London a palace as this, for here the emperor keeps all his stores of cannon, arms powder so that it rather seems the emperor's grand repository, for his wealth, his arms, himself and his family. There is this distinction that everything within these walls is extremely neat; all the walks throughout the palace are very smooth and even, most of them terraced, and several of them covered with solid work: the galleries that join the apartments, are all of mosaic work. The tiling of all the apartments are of a green color, allowable to no Buildings but the emperor's and the mosques; and there are abundance of steeples in the palace, with gilded spires and green tiling; which all together, at a distance, make a pleasant sight. The whole circumference of these Palaces may be near three or four miles, including several gardens, meadows etc..

The inhabitants are divided into the Moors, who generally inhabit the sea coast, the Arabs who generally live in tents and inhabit the Plains. The Barebbers (Berbers), an ancient race of Moors who inhabit the Mountains and seem to be the original inhabitants of this country.

The Jews who were chiefly drove from Spain and Portugal.

And lastly the Negroes who make the greatest figure in this country. These six different sorts of people make up the subjects of the emperor of Morrocco, with various complexions

Two hundred years after Leo leaves Africa in 1729

[137] The History of the Revolutions in the Empire of Morocco: Upon the Death of the Late Emperor Muley Ishmael; Being a Most Exact Journal of what Happen'd in Those Parts in the Last and Part of the Present Year. With Observations Natural, Moral and Political, Relating to that Country and People. By John Braithwaite, James and John Knapton, Arthur Bettesworth, 1729 Pg.285-350

from very fair to very black. But the negroes, at present, are the Grand Caviers of this part of Barbary:

Morocco Past and Present

Figure 56 a) 1845 Musee des Augustins b) 20th century Moorish woman c) Current king of Morocco Mohammed VI. Descendant of Mulley Ismael meeting with

[138]*Tradition and history are in accord in representing the most ancient inhabitants of the oases to have been the Berauna, a name under which the Arabs group the Negros of Bornu as well as Tebu. The oldest dynasty of the Berauna was that of the Nesur, originally from Sudan. Previous to 1811, the documents preserved by the marabouts of Traghen show that the dynasty of Uled-Mohammed occupied the throne of Fezzan for many centuries. Mr Duveyrier adduces a number of proofs to shown that the Berauna above mentioned were identical with the Garamantes, so that it becomes almost a matter of certainty that at a very ancient date a negro civilization prevailed over the northern Sahara; and that this was far advanced for its time is shown by the remains of remarkable hydraulic works, by tombs of distinct character, and by rock sculptures which record the chief facts of their history.*

By the 19th century the explorers considered Fezzan *a mixed people of Teda, Bornu, Tuareg, Berber and Arab. In color the people vary from black to pure white, the features and woolly hair being Negro. If among such a mixed people there can be said to be any national language, it is that of Bornu which is most widely understood and spoken.*

---

[138] The Encyclopædia Britannica: A-ZYM Day Otis Kellogg, Thomas Spencer Baynes, William Robertson Smith Werner, 1903 volume(F)Fezzan pg. 129-130

European Civilization *1500 AD to Present*

Figure 57 a). Alfonso VII King of Leon and Castillia under the Moorish Empire of Spain.
b).(Charles the great, Charlemagne& Carolus Magnus) from the Coronation of the king, depicted in the Sacramentary of Charles the Bald (ca. 870) Paris, Bibliothèque nationale de France, ms. Latin 1141,
c). Obverse of a Charlemagne coined in en: Frankfurt from 812 to 814, today at the en: Cabinet des Médailles in Paris.
d). king of England Athelstan on the left presenting a book to St Cuthbert to the right, illustration in a gospel book presented by Athelstan to the saint's shrine in Chester-le-Street, the earliest surviving royal Anglo-Saxon portrait (Corpus Christi MS 183, fol. 1v) Scanned from the book The National Portrait Gallery History of the Kings and Queens of England by David Williamson. Athelstan is considered the first true king of England. He was the son of Edward and a mistress.
e).Eadgyth or Edith of England (910 – 946), and her husband Otto I, Holy Roman Emperor also known as Otto the Great, who was the founder of the Holy Roman Empire, from 936 to 973. He was "the first of the Germans to be called the emperor of Italy". At the Cathedral of Magdeburg, Germany from ca. 1250 Image by Chris 73

African Christians sided with their brothers by faith, in Europe and forged a brotherhood against Islam. Merchants and evangelists, continued to flow leaving a trail of wealth and theology, which led to the building of the first castles and churches there. While the gradual transplant, ultimately led to a decline in Africa. The immigrating tribes of African moors, and Jews also forced a new distinction of European dialects.

The distinction of the French and German languages in Switzerland…The present day German took its rise from the original roots of that language. In the lands about the lakes of Geneva and Neufchatel…. the Gallo-Roman popular dialect kept its ground, from which were formed several romance dialects: from these again the Provencal: and at last the modern French.

In the North Western parts of Europe Welsh, Irish, Cornish and numerous other dialects were spoken. The popular version of history puts European people light years ahead of everyone in the world, but [139]deplorable living conditions, high mortality rates and low life expectancy plagued the region for many years. Northern tribes did not yet have the ability to read or write and most of their

---

[139] House of Commons Papers, Volume 32 Great Britain. Parliament. House of Commons H.M. Stationery Office, 1836 pg49

history comes from second hand accounts. [140]In a book titled *Letters to a Young Gentleman Commencing His Education,* Noah Webster conveys a sense of awe at the history of his kindred.

The Romans carried a knowledge of letters wherever they carried their arms and their conquests—along the Danube and the Rhine, and into Britain. But so little was this knowledge coveted by ignorant and warlike people, that for centuries after those conquests, and even after the christian religion was received, few men, even of the nobility, could write or read. The prejudice against learning, and particularly against committing the laws to writing, were not to be overcome, but by slow degrees. The Emperor Justinian, for example, assigned lands to the Lombards in Pannonia, about the middle of the sixth century; and a century passed, after that period, before they would consent to have their laws reduced to writing.

In the long period which elapsed from the first migration of the Japhetic families into Europe, to the Roman conquests in Gaul and Britain, and for some ages after, the sole business of the people was war and the chase; The young men at eighteen or twenty years of age, took the buckler, the sword and the lance, and were then obliged to seek their subsistence by the chase, or by plundering their neighbors.

It is painful to cast our eyes over Europe, and survey a population of many millions, engaged, for two or three thousand years, in making war on each other, one tribe or nation making inroads on another, slaughtering men, women and children, or expelling them from their residence, and plundering them of all their possessions. But of the fact, the concurring testimony of authors leaves us no room for doubt. The practice of plundering may have originated in the poverty and distress of nations, who had no other means of procuring subsistence ;

Yet the rude nations of Europe had such imperfect notions of right and wrong, that they maintained war to be just, alledging that force constitutes right—that the Deity intended the strong should plunder the weak, who must abandon the goods which they have not power to defend.

---

[140] Letters to a Young Gentleman Commencing His Education: To which is Subjoined a Brief History of the United States by Noah Webster Howe & Spalding, S. Converse, printer, 1823 received by Harvard college in 1879. Pg. 125-129

The knowledge of right and wrong and the defining of morality and ethics, slowly ignited in the North. [141] African missionaries reached Britain and begun to convert the Britons:

How or when the Christian religion was first introduced into Britain cannot now be ascertained. As early as the beginning of the third century the African church father Tertullian referred to the Britons as a Christian people, and in 314 the British church was recognized by the Council of Arles as an integral part of the church universal. Throughout the period of Roman control in the island Christianity continued to be the dominant religion. When, however, in the fifth century and after, the Saxons and Angles invaded the country and the native population was largely killed off or driven westward (though not so completely as some books tell us), Christianity came to be pretty much confined to the Celtic peoples of Ireland and Wales. The invaders were still pagans worshiping the old Teutonic deities Woden, Thor, Freya, and the rest, and though an attempt at their conversion was made by a succession of Irish monks, their pride as conquerors seems to have kept them from being greatly influenced. At any rate, the conversion of the Angles and Saxons was a task which called for a special evangelistic movement from no less a source than the head of the Church. This movement was set in operation by Pope Gregory I. (Gregory the Great) near the close of the sixth century.

On Whitsunday, June 2, 597, Ethelbert renounced his old gods and was baptized into the Christian communion. The majority of his people soon followed his example and four years later Augustine was appointed "Bishop of the English." After this encouraging beginning the Christianizing of the East, West, and South Saxons went steadily forward.

After the Bards and Saxons took hold of the country, we are told that the residents were pushed west; and in the mid 18th century [142]Selden says, that *the Scots inhabiting the northern parts of that kingdom, (Scotland) were called Deucalidonians, which in their language signifies as much as Black and Swarthy, as the ocean which washes the northern shore of Scotland.*

---

[141] The source book of medieval history: documents illustrative of European life and institutions from the German invasion to the Renaissance by Frederic Austin 1907 pages 72-73
[142] A Collection of Voyages and Travels, Volume 2 Awnsham Churchill Asian Educational Services, 1732 pg. 394

Then[143]Mr. Martin says that they occupied the North Western regions of Scotland and Ireland.

THE Inhabitants of this Isle are well proportion'd, generally Brown, and some of a Black Complection; they enjoy a good ftate of health, and have a genius for all Callings or Imploy-

Weftern Iflands *of* Scotland, *&c.* 229

THE Inhabitants are all Proteftants, and speak the *Irifh* Tongue generally, there being but few that speak *Englifh*; they are grave and reserv'd in their Conversation, they are accuftom'd not to bury on *Friday*; they are Fair of Brown in Complection. and use the same Habit, Diet, *&c.* that is made use of in the adjacent Continent and Isles. There is only one Inn in this Isle.

J U R A H.

THE Natives here are very well proportioned, being generally black of Complection, and free from bodily imperfections. They speak the *Irifh* Language, and wear the Plade, Bonnet, *&c.* as other Islanders.

The castles below in Jura and Skye are identical to the few remaining in Africa and the third is on a street named Dahomey in Saint Benin France.

Figure 58a)Lestat-jan mehlich Będzin Zamek b)Dunvegan Castle in Skye Mac_Leod similar to great Zimbabwe c) Compiègne tribunal de Commerce ancienne filiale de la rue du Dahomey) by P.poschadel

---

[143] A Description of the Western Islands of Scotland: Containing a Full Account of Their Situation, Extent, Soils, Products, Harbours, Bays... With a New Map of the Whole, ... To which is Added a Brief Description of the Isles of Orkney, and Schetland written By, Martin Martin and published by Andrew Bell, at the Cross-Keys and Bible, in Cornhil, near Stocks-Market., 1703 pg158-240

[144]Then also in the 18th century another observer tells us of the Jews and those still residing in Portugal and throughout Europe.

> That is the Myftery. Tis also a vulgar Error that the *Jews* are all black; for this is only true of the *Portuguese Jews*, who marrying always among one another, beget Children like themselves, and consequently the Swarthiness of their Complexion is entail'd upon their whole Race, even in the Northern Regions. But the *Jews* who are originally of *Germany*; those, for Example, I have seen at *Prague*, are not blacker than the rest of their Countrymen.

This population of Africans, moors, Romans or Jews, is well documented in Europe for many years after they were supposedly expelled from their properties. The Norman invaders took possession of everything; and expelled many out on the streets, most became destitute wanderers, others mixed in through marriage and their identity concealed itself. How and why did dark skinned people disappear? Two theories have been posited: 19th century British ethnographer/Anthropologist, David Mac Ritchie believed, that they were absorbed by an invading population. Mac Ritchie connected the traditions of face blackening and tattooing to these ancestors. He believed that the customs and traditions were all artifacts of their past communities. Mac Ritchie also says that names of areas like the Black Sea, the Black forest or people with the last names Moor or Moorison and Woodstock, corresponded to the physical descriptions of the ancient people.

Figure 59 a) stone town-Fort-Zanzibar b) Palace Gate Morroco c) 20th century post card from Marcherose or du marché rose in Bamako Niger d) A Mosque in Djenné Mali on 12-27-1972

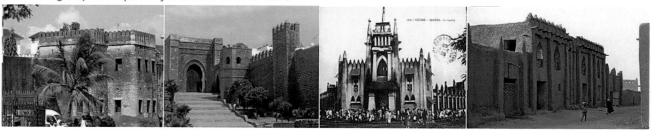

---

[144] A new voyage to Italy: with curious observations on several other countries, as: Germany, Switzerland, Savoy, Geneva, Flanders, and Holland; together with useful instructions for those who shall travel thither, Volume 1, Part 1 Maximilien Misson Printed for R. Bonwicke, 1714 pg. 139

Speaking of the Natives he states that:

[145]*The islands which were their home (in Scotland) since an ascertained epoch, are or were known to the people*

of the mainland as Inchegall or Innse-Gall, the Isles of the Foreigners, and to this day " an islander " (*innseanach*) means " an. Indian." And although the " black heathen " were expelled from these islands many centuries ago, and although, as a distinct race, they have almost vanished from Europe, yet there may be traces seen of them even yet, in the physique and the complexion of their descendants, whether in the Hebrides or elsewhere. It would be impossible to decide with certainty who are their descendants and who are not, but so far as complexion goes, the " moors " are still largely represented throughout the British Islands ; although of course the crossing and re-crossing of thirty generations, while increasing the number of descendants, has lessened the intensity of the resemblance to the ancestral stock. But the swarthy hue asserts itself still, though in a modified degree. Last century, when Martin described the *Western Islands of Scotland*, he remarked that the complexion of the natives of Skye was " for the most part black ; " of the natives of Jura he said that they were " generally black of complexion," and of Arran that they were " generally brown, and some of a black complexion." The inhabitants of " the Isle Gigay " presented a greater mixture : they were " fair or brown in complexion."✦ And Pennant, speaking of the Islay people, describes them as " lean, withered, dusky, and smoke-dried."

Also [146]*The African pygmies probably reached Europe during the Stone Ages.*

[147]But William Probert, in his book titled The Ancient Laws of Cambria 1823, said that the natives of Britain were eaten down to the bones, by the invading cannibalistic Bards and Saxons.

---

[145] Ancient and Modern Britons: A Retrospect, Volume 1 By David MacRitchie 1884

[146] The Periplus of the Erythraen Sea by a merchant of the First Century Hanno: a voyage of discovery down the West African coast Hanno Commercial Museum, 1913 Translated by Wilfred Schoff. Pg. 26

[147] This is also recorded in *Notes and queries: a medium of communication for literary men, artists, antiquaries, genealogists, etc of* 1859

The first was Gwrgi Garwlwyd, who, after tasting human flesh in the court of Edelfled the Saxon king, became so fond of it that he would eat no other but human* flesh ever after. In consequence of this, he and his men united with Edelfled king of the Saxons; and he made secret incursions upon the Cambrians. and brought a young male and female whom he daily ate. And all the lawless men of the Cambrians flocked to him and the Saxons, where they obtained their full of prey and spoil taken from the natives of this Isle. Gall, the son of Dysgyvedawg, who killed the two brown* birds of Gwenddoleu, and that daily devoured two bodies of the Cambrians for their dinner and two for their supper. The second was Ysgavnell, the son of Dysgyvedawg, who killed Edeifled king of Lloegria, who required every night two noble maids of the Cambrian nation, and violated them, and every morning he killed and devoured them. The third was Difedel the son of Dysgyvedawg. who killed Gwrgi Garwlwyd,

And this Gwrgi killed a Cambrian male and female every day and devoured them, and on the Saturday he killed two males and two females, that he might not kill on the Sunday. And these three persons, who performed these beneficial assassinations, were bards.

We will have to start from the beginning to carefully retrace the disappearance of color in Europe.

Figure 60 Map of Europe

After the Moorish invasion of 768, Charlemagne was crowned King of the Franks, King of Italy from 774, and from 800 he became the first emperor of all of Europe, also called the Father of Europe (pater Europae). He managed to unite most of Europe from the North Sea to Italy and from the Atlantic Ocean to the Danube River for the first time. He achieved his anointing in 800 AD on Christmas Day, when he was crowned "Emperor" by Pope Leo III.

[148]*He conquered the mighty Tetonic power, (of Germany) and won the imperial crown of the Western Kingdom. After him there never existed a leader amongst the Germans whose personal influence was sufficiently powerful to keep united under one scepter a great nation composed of* so many different races*. Although his great and powerful laws and institutions still continued for many centuries to be reverenced, especially amongst the Franks, still his kingdom always continued to descend in a divided form to his posterity. It was not so much the freshly awakened influence of Rome, as an impulse originating from the German people themselves, which led them to endeavor to obtain a division of races, and geographical distribution of the lands which had now became their own, and with political knowledge communicated to them by Charlemagne, to form single independent states.*

[149]*Out of the long array of Gemanic successors of Charlemagne, he is with otto III, the only one who comes before us with a genius and a frame of character that are not those of a Northern or a Teuton....and other gifts inherited perhaps from his half Norman, half Italian mother.*

---

[148] The Life of Alfred the Great Reinhold Pauli, Paulus Orosius, Benjamin Thorpe, G. Bell & sons, 1893 World history- 582 pg1

[149] James Bryce. The Holy Roman Empire (new ed. New York, 1904), pg. 207-208

The church in this era was also threatened by the persistence of impenetrable heathenism from the North.

[150]*The Vikings burst onto the scene in a flash, startling the world with the reach and extent of their raids and overwhelming destruction they wrought. Their unconventional war strategies, which left the enemy helpless and defenseless, built their reputation as brutal, bloodthirsty barbarians with no regard for God or human life. The reckless raiding of churches and monasteries was due in part to their ignorance of the unspoken rules of warfare, giving holy sites immunity, but it earned them the Christian world's contempt.*

[151]Arabian ambassador Ibn Fadlan, was dispatched to the king of the Bulgars in the 10th century. He painted the most unflattering portrait of Northern Europeans, then referred to as Vikings. They were still described among other things as: *beautiful, tall, blonde haired and blue eyed people with pale skin, but Fadlan says they were illiterate, lived in wooded homes of ten to twelve people and lacking modesty in defecation, they do not wash their hands, thus they are like wild horses.*

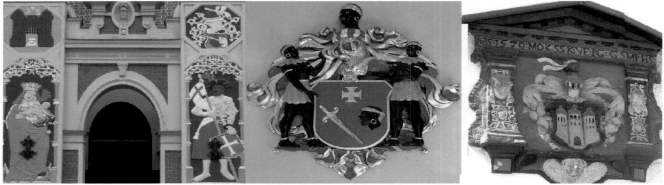

Figure 61 a). Entrance to the House of the Brotherhood of Blackheads in Riga by Brunswyk b). The House of the Blackheads in Riga. c). Eisenberg (Thuringia) Hall, coat of arms by Andreas Praefckea).

In this era, blacks lived and travelled throughout Europe as merchants, scholars, artisans and Christian soldiers. [152][153]The wealthiest families, like the Tucher, Reiter, Durer and Holper were featured as Moors on their coat of arms and these wealthy royal blacks were being depicted in renaissance art.

[154]*Penhalurik, qual. Pen-halou-rick (Head of the Rich Moors)*

[150] Norse Warfare: The Unconventional Battle Strategies of the Ancient Vikings by Martina Sprague page 308

[151] Muslim Journeys | Item #152: Ibn Fadlan's Journey to the Land of the Rus", June 05, 2013& http://bridgingcultures.neh.gov/muslimjourneys/items/show/152

[152] A Short View of the Families of the Scottish Nobility: Their Titles, Marriages, Issue, Descents; To which are Added, a List of All Those Peers who Have Served in Parliament Since the Union; By Mr. Salmon by Nathaniel Salmon W. Owen, 1759 pg87 moor's head nuwburg

[153] The Peerage of Ireland: A Genealogical and Historical Account of All the Peers of that Kingdom; Their Descents, Collateral Branches, Births, Marriages, and Issue ... with Paternal Coats of Arms, Crests, Supporters, and Mottoes ... Some Account of the Antient Kings, &c, Volume 2 by Edward Kimber, John Almon, 1768 pages 4,121,179, 210.

[154] Patronymica Cornu-Britannica: or, The etymology of Cornish surnames by Richard Stephen Charnock Longmans, Green, Reader and Dyer, 1870 pg 85

Observations on the Antiquities Historical and Monumental of the County of Cornwall (etc.)-Oxford, W. Jackson 1754 by William Borlase (Cornish English vocabulary) 402

1237 the Knights of the Teutonic Order were summoned to their aid in the conversion of the country after the fashion of the conversion of those days. The ancient towns of this land contain many curious and interesting relics of the old trading companies. At Riga is the Schwartzhaupter Haus, erected about A.D. 1200, a brotherhood of unmarried merchants called Blackheads, from their patron saint, St. Mauritius, with a very rich collection of [155] ancient plate, mostly of Hanseatic origin.

[156]The monastery in Stevenson Normandy *had an alien priory of black monks....*[157] the Justina monastery which now hold the black Benedictine monks.

Some monks and preachers like William Tyndale (1490-1536) were executed, and very little information remained of their identity,

[158]*David Baker, an English Benedictine monk and ecclesiastical historian, was born at Abergavenny, 1575. He received his early education at Christ's Hospital, in London, whence, in 1590, he went to Oxford, now Pembroke college. The latter years of his life were employed in searching after and transcribing the records of the ancient congregation of the black or Benedictine monks in England.*

Figure 62Don Fransico de Arobe and sons in European Attire. Museum in Madrid Spain

---

[155] Two Thousand Years of Gild Life: An Outline of the History and Development of the Gild System from Early Times, with Special Reference to Its Application to Trade and Industry; Together with a Full Account of the Gilds and Trading Companies of Kingston-upon-Hull, from the 14th to the 18th Century Joseph Malet Lambert A. Brown and sons; [etc., etc.,], 1891 - Guilds – pg154
[156]The journey-book of England. Berkshire (Derbyshire, Hampshire, Kent).By England 1840 pg. 125
[157] Titus Livius Patavinus, by Giacomo Filippo Tomasini, Andreas Frisius, 1670
[158]National cyclopaedia - 1879 pg707

The early Catholic Church received bishops from the African council. In the 11th century, Pope St. Leo IX, cited the significance of the bishops of ancient Numidia, his words,

[159]*now engraved in letters of gold on the modern basilica of Carthage, built by Cardinal Lavigerie: "Sine dubio, post Romanum pontificem, primus Nubiae episcopus et totius Africae maximus metropolitanus est Carthaginiensis episcopus" (There can be no doubt that after the Roman Pontiff the first Bishop of Nubia, and indeed the principal Metropolitan of Africa is the Bishop of Carthage).*

So what happened?[160]

(*) The Prince alledges several other pressing Reasons, and, in general, says that the inexpressible Cruelties of the Spanish Tyrant, excell'd those of Phalaris and Nero, &c. p. 63. That he massacred above a Hundred rich Christian Merchants among the Moors, only to Invade their Effects, p. 41. That he miserably put to Death above twenty Millions of People in the Indies, so enjoy their Estates, p. 50. That never any Tyrant has more proudly violated the Privileges of a Country, nor broken his Faith with less Shame, &c. p. 71. That Duke d'Alva has bath'd himself in the Blood of all;—That he boasts of having shed the Blood of above eighteen Thousand poor innocent Creatures by the Hand of the Publick Executioners, p. 84. 88.

Figure 63 Albrecht Dürer German painter, and mathematician Nuremberg the Irish Pot of Gold (1484–1490)

It is an incontestable fact, that there was a superfluous presence of blacks within the rising European culture. This is represented in art, music, literature, religion and language.

---

[159] What is church history?: an African perspective by Hilary C. Achunike Rex Charles and Patrick, Jan 1, 1996
[160] A new voyage to Italy: with curious observations on several other countries, as: Germany, Switzerland, Savoy, Geneva, Flanders, and Holland; together with useful instructions for those who shall travel thither, Volume 1, Part 1 Maximilien Misson Printed for R. Bonwicke, 1714 pg. 534

Italian scholar Francesco Petrarch 1304 – July 19, 1374 was kicked by a donkey. There was no discovery of new information but a revival of the old.

Petrarch characterized the era preceding the 14th century as the Dark Ages.

Modern scholars tell us that [161]*The Dark Age was a term applied in its widest sense to that period of intellectual depression in the fifth century to the revival of learning about the middle of the fifteenth... The term Dark Age became widely accepted for centuries even appearing in the American Encyclopedia of 1883.*

[162] The former ages of development were called the Dark Ages; because of the many wars, famines and epidemics; but were really an era of prevalent African occupation. This is a place in time where we are asked not to look, so the light has been left off in this room. Books, paintings and many artifacts of this time were burnt. Many of the sources from this era are second hand references.

[163] John Knox' visited France in the 18th century:

As for the fard or white with which their necks and shoulders are plaistered, it may be in some measure excusable, as their skins are naturally brown.

their faces are concealed under a false complexion, so their heads are covered with a vast load of false hair, which is frizzled on the forehead, so as exactly to resemble the wooly heads of the Guinea negroes.

the hair of our fine ladies is frizzled into the appear- of negroes wool, and stiffened with an abominable paste of hog's grease, tallow, and white powder. On

Figure 64 Charles VI, Holy Roman Emperor and his family by Martin Van Meytens 1675-1770

[164]*The (Austrian) Emperor Charles VI is of a middle stature, moderately fat, of a hale, swarthy complexion, has a brisk eye and thick lips; the latter being the distinguishing mark of the Austrian family.* [165]*Bach was then fifty nine, rather short in stature, with black hair and eyes and a brown complexion.* [166]*King James was of more than common*

[161] Petrarch's Conception of the 'Dark Ages' by Theodore E. Mommsen Vol. 17, No. 2 (Apr., 1942), pp. 226-242 Published by: Medieval Academy of America Article URL: http://www.jstor.org/stable/2856364

[162] The Jews and Moors in Spain by Joseph Krauskopf M. Berkowitz & Company, 1886 p6 19-20

[163] A New Collection of Voyages, Discoveries and Travels: Containing Whatever is Worthy of Notice, in Europe, Asia, Africa and America, Volume 5 by John Knox J. Knox, 1767

[164] Modern History Or the Present State of All Nations, Volume 2 Thomas Salmon 1745 pg.62

[165] The Present State Of Music In Germany, The Netherlands, And United Provinces. Or The Journal of a Tour Through Those Countries, Undertaken to Collect Materials for A General History Of Music: In Two Volumes, Volume 2 Charles Burney, Becket, 1775 pg.271

[166] A new and full, critical, biographical, and geographical history of Scotland: containing the history of the succession of their kings from Robert Bruce, to the present time. With a geographical description of the several counties... together with an appendix... and a map of each county in Scotland, William Duff Printed for the author, 1749 pg.128

stature, well-proportioned and stately in his person, and of a swarthy complexion. He was of a very proud and haughty mind.

[167] *King Edward the First, the black king of Wales*

Of his Perſonage and Conditions.

HE was tall of ſtature, higher then ordinary men by head and ſhoulders, and thereof called *Longſhank*; of a ſwarthy complexion, ſtrong of body, but lean; of a comely favour; his eyes in his anger ſparkling like fire; the hair of his head black and curled. Concerning

The images of the earliest Kings of England, with names like *Edward or Hugh the Black,* [168]*James Stuart the black Knight* and [169]*Ludovico Sforza the moor,* add credibility to an African presence beyond the confines of Spain.

By the 13th century, the mostly homogenous landscape of blondes and red heads was almost entirely filled with black heads. These indicate a mixture from the immigration of blacks. Their presence in Europe, leads to cultural and academic awakenings. Until the 19th century, nappy wigs and faux hair pieces became popular and dresses appear as if the women had larger hips.

Then in the mid-14th century, the Black Death spread through Western Europe and North Africa. The total number of deaths worldwide have been estimated at 75 million people, approximately 25-50 million of which occurred in Europe alone. Unsanitary conditions devastated the emerging European civilization in the 13th to 14th Century, when the Bubonic Plague ravaged the region. This epidemic and its horrific effects caused people to seek explanations and here the root of anti-Semitism was strengthened. Jews lived in separate communities and observed strict levitical customs, concerning the preparation of food and general laws of cleanliness which were centuries before their time. They may have also developed an immunity to these plagues because of previous exposure; and so their societies were preserved.

The preservation of the Jews in the face of the annihilation of Christians, raised even greater envy and jealously against them. Most of the new immigrants into Europe were probably the greatest casualties, because they had no immunity to Eurasian diseases. But they left behind all of their great wealth, which was seized by the church. This *new* wealthy and most powerful entity, functioned as the only source of order and education; and laid the foundation for the advancement of the nations. The mass slaughter of people, also stirred a sincere desire for answers. This led to a desire to learn more about the gospel and the history of the world and sparked the greatest phenomenon in the human spirit.

---

[167] Chronicle of the Kings of England: With Additions Richard Baker 1670 pg102

[168] The history of Scotland, from the year 1423 until the year 1542: Containing the lives and reigns of James the I. the to the V. With several memorials of state, during the reigns of James VI. and Charls V. William Drummond pg.47 Printed by H. Hills, for R. Tomlins and himself, 1655

[169] The history of England, Volume 1 Rapin de Thoyras (Paul, M.) J. and P. Knapton, 1743 pg717

Figure 65 Tynsdale, Luther, Calvin and Bacon

In 1439 German Johannes Gutenberg, produced a movable type printing, based on a four hundred year old Chinese invention, and the first book was printed. The Bible sparked one revolution after another and started the most enlightening period in European history. Education and the spirit of learning made its first public appearance during the 15th century, when the bible conjured a new enthusiasm. Knowledge of its hidden secrets to power were soon widely sort after.

By the 16th century, Northern and Western Europe, became further divided into many ideological toes including, Lutheran, Anglican, Calvinists, Baptists, and later Scientists. Luther translated the Bible into German and Calvin worked from Switzerland and Paris to establish his formal doctrine.

[170]*The first translation of the bible into English, by William Tyndale, 1490-1536, was printed in Antwerp, cologne, Mainz and Worms, and smuggled into England. Tyndale visited Luther in Wittenberg in 1524 and Closely followed Luther's German language bible. He was arrested and executed in 1536 leaving an unfinished work behind.*

[171]*Grammar teaching meant the teaching of Latin Grammar. Italian was the only modern language which presented anything that could be called literature. All the valuable books extant in all the vernacular dialects of Europe would hardly have filled a single shelf. England did not yet possess Shakespeare's plays, nor France Montaigne's Essays, nor Spain Don Quixote.*

Latin also facilitated international communication and research as science emerged; and so it remained an academic requirement. The Latin roots were then borrowed to form new words in English and then about a third of English came from French. Most scholarly writing was done almost exclusively in Latin, a language which ordinary people did not speak and was reserved almost entirely for the wealthy and clergy; so the illiterate masses relied on their interpretations of the obscured scriptures.

---

[170] Biblia- das ist: die gantze Heilige Schrifft Deutsch: Die Lutherbibel von 1534. Martin Luther, Stephan Füssel, Taschen
[171] Early schools and school-books of New England by George Emery Littlefield, Club of Odd Volumes
The Club of Odd Volumes, 1545 pg 231-232

Writers like William Shakespeare (1582-1616), provide a glimpse into the times, in plays like the merchant from Venice and the two gentlemen from Verona. [172]

> 240   *The Two Gentlemen of Verona.*
> *Thu.* What says she to my face?
> *Pro.* She says, it is a fair one.
> *Thu.* Nay, then the wanton lies; my face is black.
> *Pro.* But pearls are fair; and the old saying is,
> "Black men are pearls in beauteous ladies' eyes."

Africans were part of the aristocratic class and may have married into the native population.

Figure 66 Painting of William Shakespeare

Figure 67.
1.(English) Queen Charlotte Sophie: 10. Sailor or Merchant by Paul Cuffe Anbetung der Konige Dominikus:
2.Alessandro de' Medici: 11.Janssens Abraham:
3. Swedish artist Jean-Étienne Liotard: 12.Agrippine Sibyl:
4.Lorenzo Lenzi: 13. Adoration of the Kings. Many many more medival paintings by artists
5. King Edward iii   like Govert Flinck and Paul Cuffe
6.Andrea Previtali
7. 14th century tents of African bishops and missionaries.
8. Major-General in the Russian army, Anbetung der heiligen Drei Konige:
9. Portrait of Joseph Bologne Chevalier de Saint-George (1745-1799) by William Ward one of the first classical musicians and composers/ black Mozart.

---

[172] The works of William Shakespeare, by Alexander Pope 1861 volume 1 pg. 237, 240 & lxxix. Act five, scene two

As the church grew, it established schools for the development of formal education. The reformations of this era were further propelled by the writings of Aristotle which were brought into Europe.

After the moors and Jews were expelled from Europe, their advances in navigation and map making were built upon, and in 1492, Spain seemed to have struck gold. Christopher Columbus discovered land on the other side of the Atlantic, and for a short time prosperity and power followed.

[173]Scholars say that Spain and Portugal were once in the lead for world domination; but cities like Cordova where scholars and merchants once thrived, were *cursed to regress for their expulsion of the Moors and Jews*. From then on, the new European powers awakened and a path to prosperity was illuminated. The Northern armies all hastened to Africa, to reap the wealth that had been flaunted by the Africans for centuries. They carried many away, plundered, burned and destroyed.

God declares a judgment against the Africans.

Micah 3

1 And I said, Hear, I pray you, O heads of Jacob, and ye princes of the house of Israel; Is it not for you to know judgment?

2 Who hate the good, and love evil; who pluck off their skin from off them, and their flesh from their bones;

3 Who also eat the flesh of my people, and flay their skin from off them; and they break their bones, and chop them in pieces, as for the pot, and as flesh within the caldron.

4 Then shall they cry unto the Lord, but he will not hear them: he will even hide his face from them at that time, as they have behaved themselves ill in their doings.

5 Thus saith the Lord concerning the prophets that make my people err, that bite with their teeth, and cry, Peace; and he that putteth not into their mouths, they even prepare war against him.

6 Therefore night shall be unto you, that ye shall not have a vision; and it shall be dark unto you, that ye shall not divine; and the sun shall go down over the prophets, and the day shall be dark over them.

7 Then shall the seers be ashamed, and the diviners confounded: yea, they shall all cover their lips; for there is no answer of God.

Micah prophesied from approximately 737–696 BC in the time of Isaiah, Amos and Hosea.

The greatest loss was the ability to see into the future. These *children of the sun*, were able to see through it's magnificent light into time, but the sun was setting and their gifts were lost. Nostradamus recorded the last of the prophecies.

Joel 2: 1-10

2 Blow ye the trumpet in Zion, and sound an alarm in my holy mountain: let all the inhabitants of the land tremble: for the day of the Lord cometh, for it is nigh at hand;

---

[173] The Jews and Moors in Spain by Joseph Krauskopf M. Berkowitz & Company, 1886. A very concise and authentic account of the Dark Ages in Europe, the height of Spanish Power and a testament to the power of the presence of the Moors and Jews in building these nations.

2 A day of darkness and of gloominess, a day of clouds and of thick darkness, as the morning spread upon the mountains: a great people and a strong; there hath not been ever the like, neither shall be any more after it, even to the years of many generations.

3 A fire devoureth before them; and behind them a flame burneth: the land (Africa) is as the Garden of Eden before them, and behind them a desolate wilderness; yea, and nothing shall escape them.

Figure 68 a) Image of Zanzibar Palace after 1896 destruction by European fire published in La Tribuna Newspaper b) [174]That ancient, venerable castle, called Steileborg, (Christiansborg) was razed to the ground, leaving not a wrack behind.

4 The appearance of them is as the appearance of horses; and as horsemen, so shall they run.

(Diodorus the Sicilian thought that the Gauls wore their hair like a "horse's mane." Today called a "Pony Tail." The appearance of horses is intended to personify the European people as those who would seize the power to direct the global ideology)

5 Like the noise of chariots on the tops of mountains shall they leap, like the noise of a flame of fire that devoured the stubble, as a strong people set in battle array.

6 Before their face the people shall be much pained: all faces shall seem like blackness.

7 They shall run like mighty men; they shall climb the wall like men of war; and they shall march everyone on his ways, and they shall not break their ranks:

8 Neither shall one thrust another; they shall walk everyone in his path: and when they fall upon the sword, they shall not be wounded.

9 They shall run to and fro in the city; they shall run upon the wall, they shall climb up upon the houses; they shall enter in at the windows like a thief.

10 The earth shall quake before them; the heavens shall tremble: the sun and the moon shall be dark, and the stars shall withdraw their shining:

> On November 1st 1755, *All Saint's Day* while many of the 275,000 inhabitants of Lisbon were in Church an Earthquake of magnitude 8.7 hit Lisbon, Portugal. Stone buildings swayed violently and then collapsed on the population, those on the river front were drowned by a subsequent tsunami and the fleeing residences left unattended fires to ravage the city. About one fourth of the population perished. The old Mosques, synagogues, churches, and many other buildings with their Moorish architecture and street designs from the Middle Ages collapsed.

---

[174] Denmark Delineated: Or, Sketches of the Present State of that Country, Parts 1-3 Andreas Andersen Feldborg, Oliver and Boyd, 1824 pg.84

Spain and Portugal once in the lead for total possession of the New World were literally barred from the battle for American territory, leaving it wholly to the English. The African coasts where slaves were held for transport was also hit. This was interpreted by many Christians in Europe as a sign to end the trade.

Another historian explains why Spain could not retain its power, and the responsibility to carry the torch of Christianity throughout the world.

> 5. The Spaniards are zealous Catholics. In no country is there more pomp and superstitious ceremony as regards religion; and perhaps in none is there less true Christianity. Though the rest of the nation is poor, the clergy are immensely rich; and their revenues very great. The arch-bishop of Toledo, has a revenue amounting to about £ 100,000 sterling per annum. Their avarice is insatiable; especially that of the mendicant friars, who profess poverty.
> 6. The clergy use their utmost efforts to prevent the diffusion of learning, and their influence is so great, that little progress in the sciences can be made by the Spaniards [175]

Why the English were selected, may have been due to their language. Like the Grecian language, English is an *abstraction made from a collection of dialects*. From the earliest descendants of Adam, *the pygmies*, the children of Japheth, the Jewish descendants of Shem and finally the Hamites of East Africa.

[176]Webster says that the bible when first translated in German, conformed to the Teutonic language style of verses and strophes; which made it easier to commit to memory. These laws formed the foundation of the first formal laws and the subsequent base of European civilization. The first mechanically printed, mass-produced English Bible, the Geneva Bible of 1560 used this style. It soon became the most popular version available to a wide audience.

The word was now translated in such a way, that it remained the seed of every structure to follow. In the New World, the Christian ideology planted the very first universities and the top Ivy League colleges in the US were grafted. Long before the government was established, education and schools were planted.

---

[175] The Second Book of History: Including the Modern History of Europe, Africa, and Asia : Designed as a Sequel to the First Book of History Samuel Griswold Goodrich Jenks, Hickling & Swan, 1852 page 114 referenced from Encyclopædia britannica: or, A dictionary of arts, sciences, and miscellaneous literature, Volume 17 Colin Macfarquhar, George Gleig A. Bell and C. Macfarquhar, 1797
[176] Letters to a Young Gentleman Commencing His Education: To which is Subjoined a Brief History of the United Noah Webster. Howe & Spalding, S. Converse, printer, 1823 pg. 125

Harvard University	Founded in 1636 as *New College* by Calvinist (Congregationalist puritans) Motto:(Truth)
Yale University	Founded in 1701 as *Collegiate School* by Calvinist (Congregationalists) Motto: (Light and truth)
University of Pennsylvania	Founded in 1740 as *Church and Charity School of Philadelphia* as a Nonsectarian, college by Church of England/Methodists members Motto: (Laws without morals are useless)
Princeton University	Founded in 1746 as *College of New Jersey* by Calvinists (Presbyterians) Motto: (Under God's power she flourishes)
Columbia University	Founded in 1754 as *King's College* Church Motto: (In Thy light shall we see the light)
Brown University	Founded in 1764 by Baptists, founding charter promises "no religious tests" and "full liberty of conscience" Motto: (In God We Hope)
Dartmouth University	Founded in 1769 by Calvinist (Congregationalist) Motto: (The voice of one crying in the wilderness)

These fruitful founding universities, then continued to seed every other institution of higher education in the United States. This transformation from the backward barbarian, to a noble and wise civilization, is the clearest reason why we desperately needed a messiah, to save the world from its utter destruction. Two millennia later his birth is still credited for the salvation of the world.

These diverging European nations, dialects and doctrines formed the toes of our statue of Kingdoms. But Daniel says:

... as the toes of the feet were part of iron, and part of clay, so the kingdom shall be partly strong, and partly broken. And whereas thou sawest iron mixed with miry clay, they shall mingle themselves with the seed of men: but they shall not cleave one to another, even as iron is not mixed with clay. Daniel 2: 42-43
European rulers would try throughout history to unite into one but:

[177] *By the summer of 1914, the tensions between the great powers of Europe had been mounting. The continent was divided into shifting powers and rival dynasties, and the decline of the Ottoman Empire. The fact that the rulers of Great Britain, Germany and Russia were first cousins did not do anything to reduce the levels of tension.*

These were the three grandsons of Queen Victoria at the helm of the First World War.

---

[177] World at War 1914-1939by Duncan Hill

Figure 69 Medieval Landscape by Francois Dubois

As prophecy stated they *mingled themselves with the seed of men: but they shall not cleave one to another.* The governments of these European nations were led by the *seeds of Queen Victoria,* but that did not stop the nations from tearing each other apart. The next phase of history is the rock which shatters the statute and establishes a new kingdom unlike any other.

A Message to Europeans.

Figure 70 Marchesa Brigida Spinola Doria By Peter Paul Rubens (1577–1640)

1My heart is indicting a good matter: I speak of the things which I have made touching the king: my tongue is the pen of a ready writer.

2 Thou art fairer than all the children of men: grace is poured into thy lips: therefore God hath blessed thee forever.

3 Gird thy sword upon thy thigh, O most mighty, with thy glory and thy majesty.

4 And in thy majesty ride prosperously because of truth and meekness and righteousness; and *thy right hand shall teach thee terrible things*.

5 Thine arrows are sharp in the heart of the king's enemies; whereby *all people shall fall under thee*.

6 Thy throne, O God, is for ever and ever: the sceptre of thy kingdom is a right scepter.

7 Thou lovest righteousness, and hatest wickedness: therefore God, thy God, hath anointed thee with the oil of gladness above thy fellows.

8 All thy garments smell of myrrh, and aloes, and cassia, out of the ivory palaces, whereby they have made thee glad.

9 *Kings' daughters were among thy honorable women*: upon thy right hand did stand the queen in gold of Ophir.

10 Hearken, O *daughter, and consider, and incline thine ear; **forget also thine own people, and *thy father's house***;

(*within a few generations those Africans who had migrated to Europe were forgotten by their descendants.*)

11 So shall the <u>king greatly desire thy beauty</u>: for he is thy Lord; and worship thou him.

12 the daughter of Tyre shall bring gifts; even the rich among the people shall intreat thy favor.

13 The king's daughter is all glorious within: her clothing is of wrought gold.

14 She shall be brought unto the king in raiment of needlework [*birth of lace and embroidery originally sewn in Europe with gold and silver thread*]: the virgins her companions that follow her shall be brought unto thee.

15 With gladness and rejoicing shall they be brought: they shall enter into the king's palace.

16 *<u>Instead of thy fathers</u>* shall be thy children, whom thou mayest make princes in all the Earth.

From here the European queen stands in place of Tyre and the old southern Bell, she will give birth to princes (sons of kings) to rule over all the Earth. The high priests are now scientists and God says:

17 I will make thy name to be remembered in all generations: therefore shall the people praise thee for ever and ever. Psalm 45

The Scientists

From the 17th century the ideology evolved into a scientific one. Its pioneers were the Euro-American disciples of our story, the rock which destroys the statue. This rock is the solid uncompromising evidence of Science. This ideology has filled the whole world; and is recognized almost unanimously as indisputable. All nations, religions and races concede to the authority of science.

---

178 Drawing of an asteroid falling to Earth. by State Farm

Figure 71 Physicists at the Seventh Solvay Physics Conference, Brussels, Belgium, October 1933 from Smithsonian Archives From back to front and from left to right:
Auguste Piccard, Émile Henriot, Paul Ehrenfest, Édouard Herzen, Théophile de Donder, Erwin Schrödinger, Jules-Émile Verschaffelt, Wolfgang Pauli, Werner Heisenberg, Ralph Howard Fowler, Léon Brillouin,
Peter Debye, Martin Knudsen, William Lawrence Bragg, Hendrik Anthony Kramers, Paul Dirac, Arthur Compton, Louis de Broglie, Max Born, Niels Bohr,
Irving Langmuir, Max Planck, Marie Skłodowska Curie, Hendrik Lorentz, Albert Einstein, Paul Langevin, Charles Eugène Guye, Charles Thomson Rees Wilson, Owen Willans Richardson

The fathers of modern science and philosophy originate from the northern hemisphere from Europe into North America. According to the African legend, *we move along the earth like on a Giant head.*

The Northern hemisphere, as the cerebrum and most of our history has been spent around the pyramids on the brainstem in the south. This illuminates the historical process of maturity on the Earth. As our eyes have now opened.

Science is the true triumph of our journey; because for most of our time

Priyan Weerappuli

here, we have relied on divine direction through priests and prophets who spoke for God. When the sun set on these sages, the children of the 15th century begun to embrace their adoption and assumed their identity as sons of God.

Francis Bacon was first to formalize the scientific doctrine which we call inductive reasoning. The scribes who followed, navigated the dark ages of ignorance, to elucidate the intelligence within them, as a shadow of the intelligence of their creator. Many of these pioneers were also Jews including Einstein and Hinesburg. Max Planck a renowned German scientist, eloquently directed a generation to the force behind his genius. Planck continued in the paths of Newton and Bacon among other pioneers believing that both traditional religion and

[179]*natural science required a belief in God for their activities, to the former he is the starting point, and to the latter the goal of every thought process. To the former He is the foundation, to the latter, the crown of the edifice of every generalized world view.*

---

[179] 'Religion and Natural Science' (1937) In Max Planck and Frank Gaynor

Our scientific pioneers built bridges out of darkness and literally provided the illumination and technology to move and communicate information, people and products more efficiently.

Science continued branching into various concentrations; from the study of medicine and the various specialist who study the human body to those who study the earth and space. From Bacon to George Washington, this rock established a new kingdom unlike any other. These masons ensured that all men would be free to worship or not, according to their own conscience.

Scottish scientist, James Clerk Maxwell believed that

In Science, it is when we take some interest in the <u>great discoverers</u> and their lives that it becomes endurable, and only when we begin to trace the development of ideas that this becomes fascinating.

All of the discoverers and founders have one thing in common, while those who would later expel their children from the structures which they erected are complete strangers. In the very same colleges which Christian scientists founded, atheists now rule. It is this same story told in the bible of Satan created by God, becoming vain and trying to take over heaven.

This is the most remarkable fact in modern science. The very mention of the words of the ancients is scoffed and laughed at in academic circles. These are the very same circles which were a few centuries ago founded by faith. The new residents, continue in the tradition of vandals, by defacing the philosophical identity of the builders. Today many are unaware that all of these giants were theists in the highest degree. Much of their writings were theological, many studied in seminaries and aspired to become priests.

We can now begin to see our greatest scientists like prophets of antiquity, as valuable to our understanding of the world, as Moses or the Buddha. All of human history and endeavor now finds a synthesis after generations of observation. We must become as little children to see the kingdom of heaven. Matthew 18:3

Because….

It is the perfection of all God's works that they shall be done with the greatest simplicity and therefore they that would understand the frame of the world must endeavor to reduce their knowledge to all possible simplicity.' Isaac Newton

[180]*The interpretation of religion, as here advanced, implies a dependence of science on the religious attitude, a relation which, in our predominantly materialistic age, is only too easily overlooked. While it is true that scientific results are entirely independent from religious or moral considerations, those individuals to whom we owe the great creative achievements of science were all of them imbued with the truly religious conviction that this universe of ours is something perfect and susceptible to the rational striving for knowledge. If this conviction had not been a strongly emotional one and if those searching for knowledge had not been inspired by Spinoza's (intellectual love of God), they would hardly have been capable of that untiring devotion which alone enables man to attain his greatest achievements.*

---

[180]Religion and Science: Irreconcilable? A response to a greeting sent by the Liberal Ministers' Club of New York City. Published in The Christian Register, June, 1948. Crown Publishers, Inc., New York, 1954.

At the foundation of Science and the wisdom of ages is a reverence and humility, which invokes the presence of the eternal. Every branch of science, sprout forth with this dependence on providential inspiration and this ideology set the United States of America up in the frontal lobes of the Earth brain.

But the seed at the foundation, hidden beneath the soil is never visible, we can only know of its presence by the fruit. John Hanson served as the first President of the Continental Congress of America in 1781. For years the story has passed on, that he was actually a man of African descent from Balti-moore Maryland.

The wealth of obscurity surrounding a man of his stature and accomplishments, begs one to believe that the claim of African ancestry is valid. Hanson created the Presidential Seal, begun the census and postal service among many other achievements all within his one year term; but there is not a single piece of literature about him until the twentieth century, when congress acknowledges that [181]

[182] *John Hanson's name will be associated forever with laying the corner stone of our great nation.* This corner stone is obviously the stone that the builders have rejected. Hanson's state of Maryland is precisely the region which Verranzano told us which blacks with Ethiopian and East Indian or Asian features were living at the time of Verrazano's landing in the 16th century. Then the first census records expose the Hanson's as negros. There was clearly a population of Blacks in the North.

Blacks in the U.S. like in Africa and around the world owned slaves. Blacks were preferred for their skill in masonry, husbandry and their nature of servitude; but every laborer without regard to color or race initially suffered the very same circumstances.

During Washington's time an Englishman named Richard Parkinson travelled to the New World with the prospect of Land ownership and adventure. He was a guest of George Washington, and also a prospective buyer for Washington's property.

The excerpt to the right, reflect Parkinson's observations:

It is precisely the same with emigrants in similar circumstances from other countries; who are in the same manner purchased and treated as slaves. I will mention a particular instance.——A Dutchman who had lost all his property, which was considerable, and was reduced to great distress, by the war with France, met with a captain of an American ship, who offered him and his two sons a free passage into America; but at the end of the voyage the captain offered them all for sale to pay for the passage. They were bought by Messrs. Ricketts, whom I have before mentioned; who paid the captain ready money for them, and the three emigrants had to repay those gentlemen by labour for a certain number of years. The father, finding himself so wonderfully disappointed in the great expectations held out to him by the captain, proved very obstinate and would not work; and was therefore (as was usual) whipped with the cow-hide, in the same way as the negroes.

Parkinson illustrates a climate of equality which was at odds with a hierarchical system in Europe.

---

[181] A Tour in America in 1798,1799, and 1800: Exhibiting Sketches of ..., Volume 1 By Richard Parkinson and George Washington.

[182] Proceedings in the Senate and House of Representatives Upon the Reception and Acceptance from the State of Maryland of the Statues of Charles Carroll of Carrollton and of John Hanson, Erected in Statuary Hall of the Capitol: January 31, 1903 United States. Congress U.S. Government Printing Office, 1903 pg14

It is very common if you step out of your house to find a man (black or white) when you come in, to have lighted his pipe and sitting down in a chair smoking without apology. Equality there destroys all the rights of the master and every man does as he likes.

Parkinson seemed to agree with the British monarchy and the system of wealth as a measure of manhood. These principles of inequality were ultimately the reason for the separation from Britain and the basis of the new nation. But the growing sentiment in Europe and the New World was that there would be no end to discrimination. It had to be stopped and prominent philosopher's like John Locke argued

[183] *Suppose this business of religion were let alone, and that there were some other distinction made between men and men, upon account of their different complexions, shapes, and features. These persons thus distinguished from others by the color of their hair and eyes. There is one thing which gathers people into seditious commotions, and that is oppression.* [184][185]

The Constitution was adopted April 28, 1788, by a vote of sixty-three to eleven. The Federalists controlled the State until 1802. In 1812 the Hanson riots in Baltimore, caused by an attack on a Federalist newspaper office, resulted in the restoration of the State to the Federalist party. From 1820 to 1850 the State was Anti-Democratic (Whig). The American party controlled the State from 1854 to 1859. In 1860–61 the people generally were opposed to secession. The Civil War began with the Baltimore riots in 1861. From 1868 to the present time (1894) the State has been Democratic. The population of the State in 1790 was 319,728; in 1890, 1,042,390. History by Scharf.

Although Locke's arguments were taking place in England, it is clear that a major rift was taking place within the nations. America adopted a new constitution which literally excluded blacks and placed them in a new bottom class just as Parkinson, friend and guest of George Washington had advised.

A very elderly looking John Hanson in 1828 threatened to move the residents of Maryland and Delaware to Africa.

Then in 1860, Abraham Lincoln was elected president, and issued the Emancipation Proclamation in 1863. Alexander Hanson, grandson of John Hanson, played a major part in the riots. He claimed that the establishment of law and order, and the basic foundation of government had been laid by his ancestors. This was the illustrious line from Edward the Black King of Wales and the Stuart dynasty of Scotland.

Figure 72. John Hanson from the library of Congress.

[183] A Letter Concerning Toleration by John Locke J. Brook, 1796
[184] Histoire des États-Unis by Grégoire Jeanne C.F. Chamerot, 1894 pg 402
[185] History of the United States of America: 1861-1865. The civil war by James Schouler Dodd, Mead, 1899

According to Alexander Hanson:

[186]
> there is no solid ground to believe that the Saxons differed in their fundamental institutions from their German brethren, or those other hordes of northern barbarians that subjugated civilized Europe on the decline of the Roman empire, it is at least certain that these institutions were completely established long before the expiration of that period, which legal history exclusively assigns, to the reign of what we now term the common law.

Whatever the truth, America recognizes George Washington as its legitimate founder. Part of Washington's first inaugural address to Congress in April 30, 1789.

No people can be bound to acknowledge and adore the Invisible Hand which conducts the affairs of men more than the people of the United States.

Every step by which they have advanced to the character of an independent nation seems to have been distinguished by some token of providential agency; and in the important revolution just accomplished in the system of their United government, the tranquil deliberations and voluntary consent of so many distinct communities, from which the event has resulted cannot be compared with the means by which most governments have been established, without some return of pious gratitude...

These reflections, arising out of the present crisis, have forced themselves too strongly on my mind to be suppressed. You will join with me I trust in thinking, that there are none under the influence of which the proceedings of a new and free Government can more auspiciously commence. We ought to be no less persuaded that the propitious smiles of Heaven can never be expected on a nation that disregards the eternal rules of order and right which Heaven itself has ordained;

Figure 73 (1780) Portrait of George Washington and his aide William Lee in the background mounted on the horse.

and since the preservation of sacred fire of liberty and the destiny of the republican model of government are justly considered as deeply, perhaps finally, staked of the experiment...

---

[186] Publications Relative to the Difference of Opinion Between the Governor and the Council [of Maryland] on Their Respective Powers by Alexander Contee Hanson Frederick Green, Printer to the State, 1803 pg.125

The Alternate World View

The further removed we are from the ancient spirit, the closer a kin we become to the barbarian. Now we find a resurgence of the old barbaric ideology of survival of the fittest.

The stories of our history didn't actually begin to change until the close of the 19th century. This is when a new generation begun to distance themselves from their foundation and invented a new ideology. This was the evolutionary perspective of the atheists. They eventually expelled the original founders of the faith from the schools and nations they built and used their advances to interpret the book of creation.

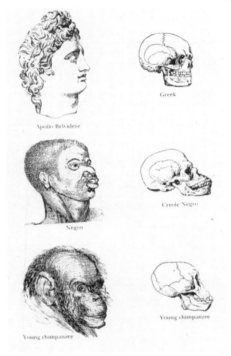

[187]Science is now the heretical system, where *scholars* have replaced the Rabbis and Popes and are now considered wiser and more capable of understanding than the average man. These scholars in place of clergy, read and interpret the world in a language too obscure for the layman.

Bacon believed that atheism was a sign of a superficial understanding. He predicted that any advancement in science would require a theistic ideology; and that a depth of knowledge in any science could not incline a man to atheism. It therefore remains that with a bit more study into history and science we would be obliged to form a similar opinion.

This leads us to create a sharp distinction here, between scientists and atheists. Science and scientist as you have seen are pragmatics, who take the road towards *personal thinking*. The Atheists' interpretation of scientific evidence, prejudicially leads towards a random, unintelligent, undirected process of development; with uncoordinated forces rather than creative genius behind them. A preference for an anthropic universe of chance and coincidence, verses an ordered, directed pattern of development.

Figure 74 A scientific demonstration by Josiah Nott a polygenist from 1868 showing the Negro to be as distinct from the Caucasian as the Chimpanzee.

One of their first prophets, French naturalist, Jean-Baptiste Lamarck, rode in on an evolving *giraffe* with a neck which mutated according to the desire of the animal. The giraffe unlike a horse or donkey is not domesticated. Its wild unsettled nature is unfit for reliable service and cannot coexist within a civilization. It is perfectly represented on the rock carvings of our earliest nomadic ancestors. Through this correlation we can see how the entire idea of modern civilization has been carefully choreographed.

Lamarck's theories which have since been discredited, formed the basis of many other theories of the disciples who followed, including Charles Darwin. Darwin is quoted with almost as much frequency as

---

[187] Exodus 7:8-12

Christ and Darwinianity is now a popular faith among scholars. Their missionaries have now implanted themselves into the education system of almost every country on earth.

A popular misconception, is that this is a no master, no God faith. According to Russian Philosopher Leo Nikolayeich Tolstoy, such a faith is impossible. Atheistic doctrine simply replaces the creator with a tangible entity that can be observed. Thereby deflecting the genius and orderly intelligence behind creation to isolated natural phenomenon. Their God is Evolution or *Luca*; a miraculous chemical concoction stirred by chance, which *coincidentally* evolves into great intelligence.

[188]The theory is, that man evolved from Apes to Africans then to whites in a gradual development towards a more *favorable race*. This vision of the African has left a subliminal, indelible mark on the dark skinned African. American students were disciplined on the hierarchy of races, and taught that Africans were closer to Apes at the bottom of the evolutionary ladder still climbing. They were *living fossils* or crude and unpolished specimens of evolution, still in process. The theory of evolution and the ascent of man cannot be separated from this vision. This theory falls apart, if we were to discover the truth of our history, so a full onslaught of geneticists, archeologists and historians, synchronize the burial of information.

The whole cavalry of eminent scholars, funded by wealthy foundations, stood in defense of a *scientific* concept of white supremacy.

[189] Their Eugenic ideology sort to exterminate all Negros from the face of the Earth. A few years later it spiraled into a holocaust in Germany and a worldwide apartheid and it continues in various forms of academic and scholarly bigotry.

Our greatest dilemma is that few are sincerely seeking an unbiased understanding of reality? Many are part of this conditioning. Speaking of science one scholar considers it [190] *a socially embedded activity* and *its change through time not necessarily a closer approach to <u>absolute truth</u>, but the alteration of cultural contexts which <u>influences what we see</u> and how we see it.*

So we must now re-examine the cultural contexts in which science has *evolved*. For the first time in our history, we are able to observe the observers, we can actually see their inherent racism impregnate the sciences; and we can trace the evolution of this bigotry, as it has been fed and nurtured into modern scholarship.

According to geneticists in Switzerland at Zurich-based DNA genealogy center, iGENEA Egyptian Pharaoh Tutankhamen (1336 BC - 1327 BC) belonged to the genetic group, known as haplogroup R1b1a2, to which more than 50 percent of all men in Western Europe belong, including 70 percent of Spanish and 60 percent of French men.

The director of the iGENEA Centre provided this interpretation:

[191]*It was estimated that the earliest migration of haplogroup R1b1a2 into Europe began with the spread of agriculture in 7,000 BC; so based on this <u>assumption</u> some claim that Tutankhamen's paternal lineage came <u>to</u> Egypt from its region of origin in Europe.*

---

[188]European traditions in the study of religion in Africa. By Frieder Ludwig, Afeosemime Unuose Adogame, Ulrich Berner, Christoph Bochinger, African Association for the Study of Religions. Page 188

[189] Race Crossing in Jamaica by Dr. C. B. Davenport, Carnegie Institution of Washington. From Scientific Monthly, September 1928.

[190]The Faith of Scientists: In Their Own Words Dr. Nancy K. Frankenberry an agnostic professor of religious studies.

[191] Aug 1, 2011 By Alice Baghdjian reuters.com/article/2011/08/01/britain-tutankhamun-dna-idAFL3E7J135P20110801

The answers put forward by these *scholars* send us back thousands of years; with many fascinating facts strung together. For one thing, if there is any evidence of agriculture in Europe around 7,000 BC how does this connect to Tutankhamen in 1500 BC?

The first historian to remark on agriculture in Europe is Herodotus; but he tells us that the *Gelonians are tillers of the ground and feed on corn and have gardens, and resemble them* (Europeans) *not at all either in appearance or in complexion of skin.* They moved north from the Hellens.

According to the biblical timeline, 7000 BC refers to the descendants of Cain and the generations before the massive tsunami recorded in Norway which triggered Noah's flood; so none of these lineages could have contributed to *haplogroup R1b1a2. (The R1b1 haplogroup is also prevalent among Africans in Cameroon and Chad.)* This analogy is equivalent to connecting today's Native Americans (who are now more genetically related to Europeans) to the founding of European civilization.

To do this, one would have to ignore all the records, images and testimonies of all the historians throughout the years, unearth a few signs of farming in America, then connect this to the development of language, writing and civilization in Europe; which is exactly what is happening here. It is clear, that there is an attempt to avoid diving into recent history. Like a cookie jar hidden far beyond the reach of a child. We are asked to search for the root of our genes, in a historical wilderness, where nothing but scraps of bones and tools can be gathered.

But we can simply go back in more relative time and ask the Egyptians, and the

Egyptians say, that many parts of the world were planted by their ancestors, by colonies sent from thence, by means of the state and [192] grandeur of their kings, and the vast number of their people.

The great population in Egypt declined precisely when the Western regions begin to be populated. [193] *Some affirm, and amongst those Ephorus, that the Idaei Dactyli had their origin from Ida in Phrygia* (A mountain in the Black Sea region of Turkey/Georgian region of the Colchis connected earlier with West African spiritual figures of Minoa and Mycenae), *and passed over with Minos* (Minoa) *into Europe; and first that brought over the rites and ceremonies of their mysteries into Greece. The Dactylic moreover, as is said, found out the use of fire, and discovered the nature of iron and brass to the inhabitants of Anti-sectarians, near to the mountain Berecynthus* (also a mountain in Turkey/Georgian) *, and taught the manner of working it: and because they were the first discovers of many things of great advantage to mankind, they were adored and worshipped as Gods: one of them, they say, was called Hercules, who was a person of great renown, and who initiated the Olympic games.*

---

[192] The Historical Library of Diodorus the Sicilian: In Fifteen Books. To which are Added the Fragments of Diodorus, and Those Published by H. Valesius, I. Rhodomannus, & F. Ursinus, translated by G Booth ESQ Harvard College Library In two volumes. Vol. 1 printed by W.M Dowall 1814 page35

[193] The Historical Library of Diodorus the Sicilian: In Fifteen Books. To which are Added the Fragments of Diodorus, and Those Published by H. Valesius, I. Rhodomannus, & F. Ursinus, translated by G Booth ESQ Harvard College Library In two volumes. Vol. 1 printed by W.M Dowall 1814 Pg. 336-341

[194]The first records of European observers gave this impression of the race of the Egyptians.

> Nigritia, and the country of the Garamantes seem, for the most part, to have been peopled at first from Egypt and Ethiopia, and consequently the inhabitants appear to have been the descendents of Misraim and Cush, though we doubt not but some colonies of Arabs likewise settled here. Some of the most perfect Egyptian mummies now remaining incline us to think, that the features of the ancient Egyptians much resembled those of the present Negroes; which is a proof that the latter must have been originally nearly related to the former. The language, or languages, therefore, spoken in these regions, bore a great affinity at first to the Egyptian, Arabic, and Ethiopic; and may at this time probably be corrupted dialects of these tongues.

Garamantes is the region of Niger, West Africa.
If language serves as a marker for race then

[195]*In addition to being used in Phoenicia, the* (Phoenician) *language spread to many of its colonies. In one, the North African city of Carthage, a later stage of the language, known as Punic, became the language of the Carthaginian Empire. Punic was influenced throughout its history by the Amazigh language and continued to be used by North African peasants until the 6th century* AD. *Phoenician words are found in Classical Greek and Latin literature as well as in writings in the Egyptian, Akkadian, and Hebrew languages.*

[196]

Figure 75 Tuareg Tribesmen from Niger West Africa a). by Marc Riboud/Magnum, As featured by the encyclopedia as a Southern Saharan Tuareg b). Modern Tuareg Clémence Delmas

---

[194] An Universal History: From the Earliest Accounts to the Present Time, Part 1, Volume 16 page174 Princeton University George Sale, George Psalmanazar, Archibald Bower, George Shelvocke, John Campbell, John Swinton C. Bathurst, **1780**
[195] http://www.britannica.com/EBchecked/topic/457164/Phoenician-languageTuareg
[196] Photograph, from Britannica Online for Kids, accessed 8/16/13, http://kids.britannica.com/elementary/art-7853.

The language is written with a 22-character alphabet that does not indicate vowels. The Phoenician writing system survived in the tifinagh script of the Tuareg, who live in the southern Sahara.

[197] *The present results support the hypothesis of a <u>recent</u> origin of modern Europeans and Caucasoids, and are clearly in favor of the <u>replacement model</u>. The time of coalescence calculated, although with a broad interval, is <u>not compatible with an origin at the time of the first hominid settlement of Europe.</u> It seems plausible therefore, given the antiquity of the first colonization that some kind of <u>population replacement occurred.</u>*

This implies that the majority of this large European population, may have been *recent* descendants of Africans. The descriptions of people in France, Portugal, Scotland and Ireland along with the English Monarchy also corroborate these findings.

In 1787, Count Constantine de Volney -- a French philosopher, historian and politician who visited Egypt, expressed amazement that the Egyptians – whose civilization was greatly admired in Europe – were not White! After visiting Egypt and studying, the structures still left behind, he deduced from the sphinx that

[198] *its features were precisely that of a Negro, I remembered the remarkable passage where Herodotus (450 BC) says:*
'As for me, I judge the Colchis's to be a colony of the Egyptians because, like them, they are black with woolly hair... When I visited the Sphinx, I could not help thinking that the figure of that monster furnished the true solution to the enigma (of how the modern Egyptians came to have their 'mulatto' appearance)

"Just think, that this race of Black men, today our slave and the object of our scorn, is the very race to which we owe our arts, sciences, and even the use of speech!
Just imagine, finally, that it is in the midst of people who call themselves the greatest friends of liberty and humanity that one has approved the most barbarous slavery, and questioned whether Black men have the same kind of intelligence as whites!

The science confirms the historical records of African, Christian soldiers and missionaries spread Christianity into Europe and evidently some of their seeds as well. In Germany the artifacts are blatant. There is a sculpture of a moor in Germany holding the Habsburgs coat of arms, in hand and his oversized genitals peeking out of his pants.

---

[197] Molecular Biology & Human Diversity. Anthony J. Boyce, C. G. Nicholas Mascie-Taylor Cambridge University Press pg. 125
[198] Travels in Syria and Egypt, During the Years 1783, 1784, & 1785, Volume 1 Constantin-François Volney R. Morison, 1801 p. 55. NOW by Joel A. Freeman, Ph.D.

These paintings referred to as the *Adoration of the magi*, were actually images of wealthy African men and their offspring?

Figure 76 a).Adoration of the Magi. Greco (1541–1614 in Prado Museum b&c. Peter Paul Rubens (1577–1640)

The assumption that Tutankhamen's paternal lineage came to Egypt from Europe, is simply not a scholarly hypothesis. These are old corruptions superimposed onto new evidence. The evidence indicates a fairly contemporary connection between Africans and Europeans, in Europe. Although the descendants have forgotten their fathers, just as the psalm predicted.

The origin of these blatant scholarly fabrications, can shamefully be linked to the Nazi ideology. When the scientific doctrine was polluted, the face of Jesus distorted; and the new image reinforced the new philosophy of racial superiority and purity. This is part of the reason why Jesus had to be connected to Egypt. Egypt has been the major contention of the ages, with a great force of scholarly reinterpretation.

George Andrew Reisner's 1908 findings are consistent with all of the facts procured in this volume.

[199]*There is not a bit of evidence pointing to a foreign race. (90)*

It has often been urged that writing was not an Egyptian invention or that it was brought into Egypt by so called Pharonic Egyptians in a comparatively perfect state. But an investigation of the known facts does not bear out either conclusion. On the contrary a comparison of the earliest writing with the pictures and reliefs of the predynastic period shows plainly enough that hieroglyphic writing is an Egyptian invention and that the dynastic people inherited writing from their racial forebears of the predynastic period. (123)

It is, I believe, impossible to escape the conclusion that the inhabitants of Egypt from the earliest predynastic period down to the end of the protodynastic period, form one continuous race and that we are here witnesses of the steps by which they conquered the stubborn materials of the Earth and earned that civilization which we call Egyptian. 135

---

[199] The Early Dynastic Cemeteries of Naga-ed-Dêr, Volume 2 University of California. Hearst Egyptian Expedition, George Andrew Reisner, Arthur Cruttenden Mace, Albert Morton Lythgoe, Dows Dunham Hinrichs, 1908 - Naga-ed-Dêr (Egypt)

The *New* face of king Tut.

Figure 77 a).A new redesigned face of Tut stands in place of the old sculptures left by the Egyptians. 2. Mummified remains of king Tut b&c Egyptian Sculptures of Tut in the color of Ra (in real life or alive in the sun) and the idealized image of Min as his (KA) to be regenerated into. Images by Jon Bodsworth

But in 1923, William Matthew Flinders Petrie (who believed that the culture of Ancient Egypt was derived from an invading Caucasian *Dynastic Race*,) was knighted for services to British archaeology and Egyptology. His excavation systems are still used by archaeologist today.

As a dedicated follower of Eugenics, Petrie believed that the *fine* Caucasian race must have conquered the *inferior* race and inhabited Egypt. Then slowly introduced the finer Dynastic civilization as they interbred with the *inferior inert race.*

[200] *His explanations of the cultural development of ancient Egypt, followed the trends of his time. Based on Darwin's theory, archaeologists developed an evolutionary approach, which made a developmental distinction between races and cultures.*

This became the clearest mark of the direction which scholarship would follow. It was an obvious sign to all of the so called scholars that the facts would have to match this picture. The facts which didn't, were frequently omitted or as in the *new* face of Tut, reconstructed, but these omissions together add up to an entirely different story.

Petrie was forced to revise his theory that Egyptians were simply Caucasians who painted themselves in dark colors, after he excavated the grounds of Egypt and found evidence of Egyptians, from the Roman Era. These attest to a still dark skinned, curly haired, Egypt even after 800 years of intermixture. Then came this theory of a *Northern invading dynasty,* which Reisner may have had to concede to.

The Northern and Western colonies in Europe had no writing and so no records, drawing or stories, concerning invading the inferior Africans. We can clearly see that an indigenous people from Africa raised the pillars of civilization in Egypt, which is in Africa.

[201] *The comparison of the Nubian ceramics found in the tombs with clearly dated predynastic Egyptian ceramics allowed precise determination of its period.*
The author estimates that, proof is now established that Nubian monarchy is the oldest in the history of humanity.

---

[200] Egyptian Archaeology, (A summation of the theories proposed by William Matthew Flinders Petrie) by Willeke Wendrich/ John Wiley & Sons, Sep 26, 2011 pg. 1988
[201] Civilization Or Barbarism: An Authentic Anthropology By Cheikh Anta Diop, Chicago Review Press, Apr 1, 1991 4th chapter

We thus understand the matriarchal essence of Egyptian royalty and the importance of the role of the queen-mother in Nubia, Egypt, and the rest of Black Africa. The women, the queen was the true sovereign, the keeper of the royalty and guardian of the purity of the lineage. To this end, it often happened that she marry her brother or her half-brother by the same father; it was she who transmitted the crown to her husband, who was only her executive agent.

In the 21st century, the identity and culture of the Egyptians and their relationship to the still obviously Negro people of Ethiopia and Sudan is continuously minimized. National Geographic Contributing Writer Robert Draper in a report titled *The "Black" Pharaohs.*

The "black" Nubians were intermingling and sometimes intermarrying with their Egyptian neighbors to the north. (King Tut's own grandmother, the 18th-dynasty Queen Tiye, is <u>claimed</u> by some to be of Nubian heritage.)
Why:
Not because the two lands were then governed as a whole and so shared customs religion and education, but because according to this *scholar*:
The Egyptians didn't like having such a powerful neighbor to the south, especially since they <u>depended</u> on Nubia's gold mines. So they <u>installed</u> Nubian chiefs as administrators and <u>schooled</u> the children of favored Nubians at Thebes. <u>Subjugated</u>, the elite Nubians began to embrace the cultural and spiritual customs of Egypt—venerating Egyptian gods, particularly Amun, <u>using</u> the Egyptian language, <u>adopting</u> Egyptian burial styles and, later, pyramid building.

The report also tried to draw distance with Reisner who is claimed to have:
besmirched his own findings by insisting that black Africans could not possibly have constructed the monuments he was excavating. He believed that Nubia's leaders, including Piye, were light-skinned Egypto-Libyans who <u>ruled over the primitive Africans</u>. That their moment of greatness was so fleeting, he suggested, must be a consequence of the same <u>leaders intermarrying with the "negroid elements."</u>

This is the root of racism and bigotry. It is taught in schools throughout the US. The religion of evolutionary supremacy is now our prevailing theology. The *fittest,* now claim to have simply been lucky to have superior stock. This is a most intellectual attempt to keep people in confusion and darkness.

It is evident, that Africans did colonize Italy and then expanded their territory further west. This explains why European civilization is relatively recent, Europeans only recently formalized their own languages and developed writing. Their buildings are also recent constructions and *recent,* becomes the resounding theme.

When coupled with recent findings that modern Europeans only became fairer in recent times, evidence of selection pressures begin to surface. By the end of the dark ages, there was probably little color left in Europe; but the imprint of their recent Negro ancestry was still very evident in the few images which remain. David Mac Ritchie's impression of his fellow Brits now makes sense. Other historians tell us of blacks throughout Europe.

Figure 78 a) Mid-19th century soldier b)later 20th century soldier assumes the identity and property of earlier soldier.

[202] *Their countenance resembling those of their race who:*

are to be met with in England; of brown complexions, and for the most part having beautiful and regular features; their eyes fiery and intelligent; their hair, somewhat coarse, of coal black hue; and all having the same free and independent bearing.

There is, however, another class of Zingani, whose very existence will surprise those who have been accustomed to consider these people as mere wandering barbarians, incapable of civilization, and unable to appreciate the blessings of a quiet and settled life; for many of them inhabit large and handsome houses in Moscow, appear abroad in elegant equipages, and are scarcely to be distinguished from the upper classes of the Russians, unless, indeed by possessing superior personal advantages and mental accomplishments.

These wandering blacks are the very descendants of those whose estates and properties were confiscated.

---

[202] The Circassian chief by William Henry G. Kingston 1843 Page 274

[203]Cosma calls the coast of Africa, which is beyond the strait of the red sea, Zingion, The inhabitants of that coast, as the father de Montsaucon observes, call it still Zingui, from whence comes the name Zanguebar, the Terra Firma of the Zangui.

Zanzibar is also an island off the coast of Tanzania in East Africa.

This corroborates an African presence in Europe, while the Egyptians in the era of Tutankhamen do not depict any European people. *Europeans are here*, but they are not as pale and their hair is not as straight. This is why all of the people who encountered the Northern army, saw a great people like no other in the world.

Jeremiah 46: *24* tells us that the d̲a̲u̲g̲h̲t̲e̲r̲ of Egypt shall be c̲o̲n̲f̲o̲u̲n̲d̲e̲d̲; she shall be delivered into the hand of the people of the north. (MtDNA represents genes from the mother's side.)
Some of the soldiers and teachers were likely African women like the Amazon women described by Herodotus. Leo also said that many wealthy kings in Africa gave their daughters to traders.

[204]The (mtDNA) Haplogroup L (excluding the derived L3 branches M and N) show no signals of having evolved within the European continent, an observation that is compatible with a recent arrival from the African continent. To further evaluate this issue, we analyzed 69 mitochondrial genomes belonging to various L sub lineages from a wide range of European populations. Phylogeographic analyses showed that ~65% of the European L lineages most likely arrived in rather recent historical times. However, the remaining 35% of L mtDNAs form European-specific sub clades, revealing that there was gene flow from sub-Saharan Africa toward Europe.

Figure 79 Magaurite or Margo, Mary Stuart of France, Anne of Denmark, Elizabeth of England

Notice the wooly hair. The woman selects the king.

It is now impossible to believe that Europeans had been living in Europe for 30,000 years, while the story of such a great civilization is barely six hundred years old. This is why Bacon says that the opinions of atheists and evolutionists imply a superficial knowledge.

---

[203] The History of the Works of the Learned, Or, An Impartial Account of Books Lately Printed in All Parts of Europe, Volume 9 by H. Rhodes, 1707 The commission of Cosma of Egypts Christian Typography. 131-134
[204] Reconstructing ancient mitochondrial DNA links between Africa and Europe. María Cerezo & Antonio Salas et al. Unidade de Xenética, Departamento de Anatomía Patolóxica e Ciencias Forenses, and Instituto de Ciencias Forenses, Facultade de Medicina, Universidade de Santiago de Compostela, Santiago de Compostela, 15782 Galicia, Spain.

My most perplexing question, was, why the scholars were fighting to lay claim on Egypt, when the monuments and history and very essence of the Egyptians, breathes true of all Africa. It only became clear when I shifted my lens to Europe and found nothing but darkness. It was then I knew that I had to revisit Italy and Greece and every story ever told. It was not enough to have robbed an entire continent of their land, their livelihood, evict people from their homes, but their history their stories, their achievements. Negros stood alone as every ethnic group found some mention in the story.

This is the *thorn in the flesh* according to Paul, *lest any of us should be exalted beyond measure,* our true story condemns any self-righteousness. From Adam's fall to Noah's drunkenness, Moses' impatience and anger, David' adultery, the foul mouths of the apostles, Peter's denial and Paul's first condemnation, a little humility is reserved for each of one of us. This is the entire theme of grace and salvation, which causes the saved to see the dignity and worth in the most unpolished, barbaric heathens.

In the second chapter of *Ephesians,* Paul asks us to remember our past before the gospel. We are forced to acknowledge the supplement responsible for our conversion from darkness, so that none of us can boast of natural strength.

2 Wherein in times past ye walked according to the course of this world, according to the prince of the power of the air, the same spirit that now worketh in the children of disobedience:

3 Among whom also we all had our conversation in times past in the lusts of our flesh, fulfilling the desires of the flesh and of the mind;

4 But God, who is rich in mercy, for his great love wherewith he loved us,

5 Even when we were dead in sins, hath quickened us together with Christ, (by grace ye are saved;)

6 And hath raised us up together, and made us sit together in heavenly places in Christ Jesus:

7 That in the ages to come he might shew the exceeding riches of his grace in his kindness toward us through Christ Jesus.

8 For by grace are ye saved through faith; and that not of yourselves: it is the gift of God:

9 Not of works, lest any man should boast.

11 Wherefore remember, that ye being in time past Gentiles in the flesh, who are called Uncircumcision by that which is called the Circumcision in the flesh made by hands;

12 That at that time ye were without Christ, being aliens from the commonwealth of Israel, and strangers from the covenants of promise, having no hope, and without God in the world:

13 But now in Christ Jesus ye who once were far off are made nigh by the blood of Christ.

14 he is our peace, he hath made both one, and hath broken down the middle wall of partition between us;

17 And came and preached peace to you which were afar off, and to them that were nigh.

18 For through him we all have access by one Spirit unto the Father.

19 Now therefore ye are no more strangers and foreigners, but fellow citizens with the saints, and of the household of God;

20 And are built upon the foundation of the apostles and prophets, Jesus Christ himself being the chief corner stone;

21 In whom all the building fitly framed together grows into a holy temple in the Lord:

22 In whom ye also are built together for a habitation of God through the Spirit.

The stark contrast between the gruesome, ferocious vandals, who destroyed kingdoms and inspired fear and revulsion from more advanced nations, to the dominant, civilized power of the world, cannot be separated from this gospel. This is the hope we possess for our mission to save the world.

Same War New Soldiers

We can almost sympathize with the new scholars. They didn't want to connect the fallen African civilizations with their former period of glory; and desperately needed to find a better beginning of their own.

By the time of the European scramble for Africa in the 19th century, Africa had suffered several crushing blows. There was the mass depopulation, prompted by the emigration, of the most able men and women from the continent. Then, a significant reduction in demand for African products, as a result of the discovery of the New World; and a route to the East which literally cut off the African middle man. Unlike the new American colony, which broke its umbilical connection to Britain; the African nations were plundered in the form of taxes, to sustain the European countries which had limited resources but escalating industrial needs. Then the demand for gold plummeted during the American gold rush, while ivory a secondary staple became outlawed. The wealthy business men also carried their wealth north, leaving the continent in continuous disrepair. Then finally Europeans had more advanced weapons, which eventually led to their success over the Africans.

In Noah Webster's Letters to young gentlemen, he illustrates this long attachment to arms among the barbarians. He shows through history, how this custom has been replaced by civility and order and in our age we can still see this ancient and most savage connection to weapons.

By the end of the 19th century and well into this past century, the ascension of blacks from the apes was all the leverage needed to justify a planned takeover of Africa. Africans were marked for extinction, and those who remained would have been sent into reserves like the natives of America and Australia; but unlike Native Americans there were three obstacles.

Figure 80 Battle of Isandlwana by Charles Edwin Fripp (1854–1906)

AFRICA: Its Colonizability by white peoples. — The regions habitable by Europeans.

— "There are three obstacles to the white race from Europe overrunning and colonising the continent of Africa as it has overrun and colonised the two Americas and Australasia. The first is the insalubrity of the well-watered regions and the uninhabitability of the desert tracts; the second is the opposition of strong indigenous races; and the third, of quite recent growth, is a growing sentiment which is increasingly influencing public opinion, in Europe more especially, and which forbids the white man to do evil that good may come: namely, to displace by force of arms pre-existing races in order that the white man may take the land they occupy for his own use. It is probable that the second and third reasons combined may in future prove the more effective checks.

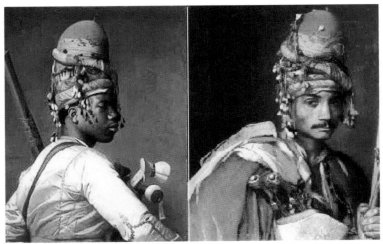

Figure 81 Bashi-Bazouk Soldiers in 1869 by Jean-Léon Gérôme (1824–1904)

Ethnic cleansing was not isolated to Africa. In the mid 1800's, the Russian government eliminated 90% of the population of Circassians, (approximately 1-1.5 million people) in the Black Sea region of the ancient colchis. This is one of the first genocides in modern history. [206]Kurds, Arabs and Nubian solidiers, called Bashi-Bazouks came together to fight against the Russian massacre.

Between 1904 and 1907, Russian scientist Ivan Pavlov discovered psychological tools for conditioning animals.

His research may have coincidently facilitated the mass manipulation of humans.

The Herero Genocide took place shortly afterwards, in the German held region of Namibia. German general Lothar von Trotha, drove the Namibians into the desert, where it is estimated that more than 80,000 people died of thirst.

---

[205] History for Ready Reference: From the Best Historians, Biographers, and Specialists; Their Own Words in a Complete System of History. Josephus Nelson Larned, Alan Campbell Reiley C.A. Nichols Company, 1910 africa pg3.
[206] The History of the War with Russia: Giving Full Details of the Operations of the Allied Armies, Volume 5 byHenry Tyrrell London Print. and Publishing Company, 1855 - Crimean War, 1853-1856 118

Figure 82 a) Herero fugitives b) Armenian corpses c) Jewish corpses

The Herero people will have to leave the country. Otherwise I shall force them to do so by means of guns. Within the German boundaries, every Herero, whether found armed or unarmed, with or without cattle, will be shot. German General

These exterminations were so successful (in that the world turned a blind eye to the killings), that they were later carried on against Armenians, in the spring and summer months of 1915. [207] *Death in its several forms—massacre, starvation, exhaustion—destroyed the larger part of the refugees. The Turkish policy was that of extermination under the guise of deportation.*

Jews in Germany, were the next targets and just thirty years later *millions* were executed from Germany. In Bosnia and Herzegovina almost 100,000 people were killed between 1992–1995. Then in 1994, the East African nation of Rwanda, once held by Germany, had a similar event. These serial killings, or tribal conflicts seem like isolated events, but it may not be that simple. Scientists have discovered conditioning techniques which influence the psyche of individuals, and probably, entire groups of people. Today, Arabians in Darfur, Sudan are attempting to wipe out the indigenous population.

Suddenly the continent was invaded by men who seized their gold and iron industries and took the most fertile land for themselves. Africans refused to work for any amount of money and forced Europeans to bring in thousands of East Indians. The continuous battleground prompted Ghandi to request the British permit the Indians to aid in the war; but Later Gandhi realized that it was *no war but a man hunt.*

Overnight masters were slaves, at home and abroad and unlike any other empire in history, segregation and racism ensured that these lines of power and poverty could never be crossed. What was taken with arms is retained with diplomacy.

Generations later, the spirit of many Africans remain shackled. Words now subjugate the minds more than any weapon could, and the subjects are educated in this vision; so that the world is thoroughly defined by it. The lines of racial discrimination eventually extended enough, to include the Irish, Italians, Jews and Hispanic, who were once outside of the definition of white. If it were not for this same gospel and this large percentage of Europeans who now pass as *white,* Negroes would have been exterminated.

---

[207] Morgenthau, Henry (1918). Ambassador Morgenthau's Story. Garden City, New York: Doubleday.

While we celebrate the tenacity and courage of activists like Martin Luther King, and Nelson Mandela, the abolition of slavery and the fight for equality would have been impossible without the brotherhood, first established among blacks and whites. We can only compare it to the feeling that Moses had, watching the Egyptians hurt people, he probably didn't know that he was related too. That same spirit of intolerance of evil, took hold of the vast number of whites around the world, at a point where they had nothing to gain from embracing equality.

Figure 83 a) Harriet Beecher Stowe 1854 by Alanson Fisher, b) William Wilberforce, e) Jacques Pierre Brissot, d) Samuel Sewall, e) John Brown, f) Abraham Lincoln

Activists like Harriet Beecher Stowe, a Connecticut teacher, who used her class room to teach the evils of slavery and wrote books on the subject.

[208]*Freedom is attended by intelligence, industry, and prosperity: and slavery brings with it ignorance, indolence, and poverty. Nothing shows this to be true so clearly as the contrast between the present condition of the great state of Virginia and the small state of Massachusetts. Both were settled by people from our country, and nearly at the same time. .*

Stowe's anti-slavery novel Uncle Tom's Cabin published in 1852, literally laid the foundation for Civil War. Uncle Tom's Cabin was the second best-selling book of the 19th century, after the Bible. The novel sold 300,000 copies in the United States and one million in Great Britain within the first year.

William Wilberforce was a politician, and influential Member of Parliament in England; who lead the movement to abolish the slave trade. Jacques Pierre Brissot founded an anti-slavery group Society of

---

[208] A New Geography for Children by Harriet Beecher Stowe Sampson Low, 1855 pg 135

the Friends of the Blacks, in Paris. Samuel Sewall (March 28, 1652 – January 1, 1730) was a judge, businessman, and printer in the Province of Massachusetts Bay, and served as the chief justice of the Massachusetts Superior Court. Sewall published the first known anti-slavery tract in America and John Brown and Abraham Lincoln both gave their lives for the freedom of blacks.

The very long list of those who supernaturally sided with Blacks against people who looked more like themselves, is astounding; especially since the institution of slavery and social castes existed in Africa among Africans at the same time. The difference has been ideology ever since the 8th century. This is the reason for the attack on religion, the one weapon which united people of all races against evil. It is important now more than ever, to identify this evil, as it subconsciously seeps into the hard drives of our thinking and destroys us like a virus. The old weapons have transitioned from spears and lances, to fire arms and now diplomacy. But with just a change of front, the enemy once in the lead is now left behind. This is our long awaited revolution.

Against all odds, we have seen Africans who were just a few generations ago were cursed by their skins, excel in almost every industry.

Just thirty years after emancipation, African American surgeon, Daniel Hale Williams opened Provident Hospital in 1893. He then became the first physician to successfully complete open-heart surgery on a patient. Many have heard of Florence Nightingale, a pioneer in nursing and humanitarian aid, but few have heard of Jamaican-born, Mary Jane Seacole (1805 – 14 May 1881), who set up a 'Hotel' behind the lines during the Crimean War for wounded officers. This was the era of the Bashi-Bazouk soldiers who probably found little aid or attention because many were Africans.

Others like Lewis Howard Latimer are associated with the most revolutionary inventions of all time: the incandescent electric light by Thomas Edison and the telephone by Alexander Graham Bell. Latimer also

published the first technical description of incandescent lighting. The period of enlightenment did not exclude African Americans just loosed from bondage, and still learning to read. Phyllis Wheatley was only a teenager when she published her then famous poetry.

[209]*Charles Henry Turner designed apparatuses (such as mazes for ants and cockroaches and colored disks and boxes for testing the visual abilities of honeybees).Turner may have been the first to investigate Pavlovian conditioning in an invertebrate. Through his observations Turner was able to establish that insects can modify their behavior as a result of experience.*

Figure 84 Charles Henry Turner

These great contributions rarely receive a place in text books and are only spoken of every February in America, so as to keep the lines in place. For centuries, students have reenacted Shakespeare's plays, and Mozart's concertos, studied Picasso's art and Freudian psychosis, while hypnotized by global conditioning techniques, to associate genius with European; and all evil with black. Educators acknowledged and celebrated the contributions of one group within the national context, while systematically erasing the

---

[209] http://www.britannica.com/EBchecked/topic/1471795/Charles-Henry-Turner

paint and obscuring the contributions of the others. Africans are featured as the dispensable extras in the story, while every single role in history has been filled by the European.

We can think of Africans as an integral part of the foundation of American history, with names like Otis and sayings like *The real McCoy*, our traffic lights, electronic control devices for guided missiles, the pacemaker, and shoemaking machines, which are just a few of their contributions. James West developed the foil electric microphone, an inexpensive, compact device in 1962 while working with scientists at Bell Labs. This device is now used in most microphones—from telephones to camcorders to baby monitors. Other scientists, artists and athletes have dramatically transformed the American identity and culture. There isn't a place in history, where the contributions of blacks has not been tainted with prejudice and condescension. Their early doctors, were *witch doctors,* even when many of their methods were copied. From Africans, the world received anesthesia, from the zombifying of people in Africa and Haiti, we learnt that the heart could be stopped to perform surgery and when a CIA chopper landed among the Azande people of central Africa in the Congo, one of the officers says:

[210]*I was lying about 20 meters from a stream, covered with bees.* (he had suffered burns to 35 percent of his body) *The villagers fashioned a crude stretcher from tree limbs and began the walk back to their village.*

I remember being washed with warm water and someone cleaning my burns with a knife. The bees were gone, but smaller worm-like bugs had gotten into my burns. Except for my hands, they were easily dealt with. Whoever it was systematically dug out every bug he could see. The effort had predictable results on the extensor tendons of my fingers. Many

were cut and no longer function. (I am not complaining. I still have fingers that work, and I can still play tennis, so I will always be grateful to that individual.) When my wounds had been thoroughly cleaned, someone applied a grease or salve-like substance onto all of my burns. It turned bluish black, hardened, and became a sort of protective coating over my burns. Essentially, it prevented both infection and dehydration--the greatest dangers for someone who has suffered severe burns. There is little question that this treatment saved my life.

Figure 85 Village chief Faustino, who helped this office.
Photo courtesy of the author

When the officer arrived in Texas, he was examined by a young Army plastic surgeon, and sent straight to intensive care with the initial odds of survival at 30-70 percent.

A steady stream of visiting doctors were interested in learning about the treatments used by the Africans. Several months later, two Air Force doctors were sent to Africa to investigate the substance used.

---

[210] Lessons in Intelligence Sharad S. Chauhan APH Publishing, Jan 1, 2004 A Compilation Of Articles From Various Sources-Relating To The Success And Failures Of Cia In Field Of Intelligence. The Study Is Divided Under 60 Headings Relating To This Sensitive Subject. https://www.cia.gov/library/center-for-the-study-of-intelligence/csi-publications/csi-studies/studies/winter99-00/art2.html

The story of this officer's burn, serves another purpose here. We notice that to heal him, the bugs needed to be pulled out, the wounds cleaned and then a new paste was placed to protect him. We can't erase racism without systematically pulling these bugs or errors from our badly wounded identity. It is impossible to tell this story without invoking some shame. We may lose some fingers or toes in the process, but we cannot undo the damage which has been done, with a simple hand shake.

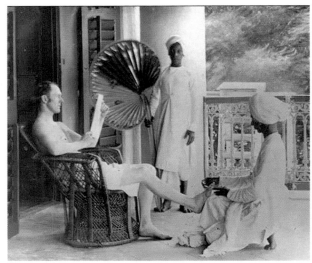

Figure 86 European invasion of India

While professing to be friends, a new godless generation continue subtle attacks on the consciousness of the people. The Northerners, now see those who are different from themselves. They are like beasts, with dark features and curly or wooly hair.

Imagine, a gang of robbers, from the ghettos around your gated communities and fenced homes, all banding together to enter your homes and confiscate your property. Suddenly your livelihood is taken from you. You are destitute and famished, and barred from every industry. Then after everything is taken, your children, are educated to believe, that they came from nothing. They tell them that they built your homes, they are the owners of your property, but they do not have the deed. They forget to take down the

Figure 87 Depiction of Early humanlike Ape. Archaeology Museum in Germany Photo by Lillyundfreya derivative of Rafaelamonteiro80

portraits hanging on the walls and your family initials still scribbled on the doors. Even with nothing left, the children still have their story, one that has been passed down as a family heirloom. A story that, awaits this very world of diplomacy.

[211]The most poignant illustration of this story, can be discovered through Nelson Mandela and the Ndebele or Matabele people of South Africa. After Mandela's death, the world reported that he was the first *Black* President of South Africa. A title of honor; but with a peculiar distinction. In a few generations we can see how this title serves the purpose of erasing the history of Blacks in South Africa. Their previous history of kings and wealth is concealed beneath the familiar story of European conquests and subjugation of the world.

This perpetuates the image of the indolent and ignorant ape.

Frank W. Sykes, C. G. Löwinger, and Archibald Constable, were part of the colonial efforts in South Africa in 1897, and tell us a different story. The people were not savage, but had

---

[211] Eleven Years in Central South Africa By Thomas Morgan Thomas Psychology Press, 1872

the tact and deliberation of their predecessors. Their patient pondering, changed the all too familiar story of white oppression and the strong plundering the weak.

> When the B.S.A. Company laid armed hands upon the Matabele nation, they merely surprised them into an apparent submission, and believing the effect of the *coup d'état* to be final, proceeded to administer the land upon the basis of a white dominant race and a heliot nation of conquered blacks. But the Matabele were not conquered, far from it, neither did they in the smallest degree consider themselves so. With the dissimulation of all negro people they remained passive, summing up meanwhile the possibilities in view of the new order of things which they had now been forced to take into account.
> Lobengula is said to have admonished his wayward nation in these terms: " Be patient and be watchful ; wait your opportunity." The first seeds of the crop of [212] horrors of 1896 were sown ;

The natives gathered together in an open revolt to reconquer their country. These revolts continued with the imprisonment of Mandela for 27 years from 1963. Around the same time that, Martin Luther King was assassinated in the U.S in 1968. Finally in 1994, Nelson Mandela was elected the first *black President* of South Africa. Around the world the battle continues, but many like Josiah are not sure which side they are fighting on.

Politicians who had lost the battle to continue slavery, adopted a new national motto; so the struggle towards equality was buried and the new scientists begun the campaign to justify a different kind of segregation. It is the intellectual warfare which we have since been engaged in; and survival is now reserved for the fittest. The strong embrace the old theology, that force constitutes right, and the strong should plunder the weak if they have no power to defend themselves.

The scholars continue the same abuses and error with a bit more tact and linguistic discretion. The very same message is choreographed with words like subjugated, installed and other derogatory terms which are intended to maintain this place of Africans in history.

But in any closed system, including history, nothing can be added or removed without changing the result. We can't simply erase something, it has to be substituted. So we can't discard the ancient records, we must substitute our understanding of history with something else. In this case, those who were without a voice or input in the ancient archives are the very people now asserting their significance. The ancients are now apes and the bible which has been at the foundation of modern civilization is removed from schools and replaced with new theories.

We can now examine the two stories side by side.

---

[212] With Plumer in Matabeleland: An Account of the Operations of the Matabeleland Relief Force During the Rebellion of 1896 Frank W. Sykes, C. G. Löwinger, Archibald Constable, 1897 - Zimbabwe

In the new story, European people took a *"great leap forward"* and ascended out of the African Abyss. Through an acquired intelligence and a series of adaptations and mutations, they developed a mastery of the elements. They became the *superior mutants, while* the primitive Africans waited patiently for their return into Africa to educate them. In this case the African who has occupied much of human history is erased. He must become an ape, and now robbed of his home and his livelihood, he must also relinquish his history and identity. His place of honor is now diminished so he must trade places with the barbarian.

The truth is there is no us and them, we are them and they are us. We speak the same language, and are the same people who separated out of Egypt, some of us have mixed with the vandals others are mixed with the slaves and many other combinations; but we are children of one God. We have continued to build empires and subsequently destroy them, through our tendency to self-destruct. Imagine now that DNA evidence infers that Hitler, was probably a Jew. Those "whites" who were most oppressive to blacks were often the ones genetically nearest to them. Yes we destroy ourselves, those who seem foreign and alien are actually our kindred.

Africans sold Africans, Africans enslaved Africans, and Africans robbed, killed and destroyed their own neighbors. Among *Europeans there are still many vandals of the unmixed and ancient composition.* The real jest of our story is that we can't identify any one else as our enemy but ourselves.

Colonial distortion of West Africa.

Figure 88 a).Soldier on Horse World Museum Liverpool, England
b).Head of a king oba, Nigeria, Benin kingdom; Brass; Africa department, Ethnological Museum, Berlin, Germany,
Inv. No. III C 8169 (Eduard Schmidt, acquired in 1898)
c).West African Door with Lock/ Brooklyn Museum
d).The Head of West African Ife bronze casting of a king image by Saiko British Museum reference Af1939, 34.1
e).Mask of Ivory, iron, and copper: Iyoba, Edo, Court of Benin The Metropolitan Museum of Art, New York, The Michael C.
Rockefeller Memorial Collection, Gift of Nelson A. Rockefeller, 1972 (1978.412.323)

Figure 89 Portrait of Diallo by William Hoare (1733)

Africans were neither backward nor primitive, their art was simply not considered beautiful and their marks of genius erased, overlooked, misrepresented, distorted or stolen.

One of the greatest artists of all time, Pablo Picasso [213]*was infatuated with African totems. Even in 1910, he was already filling his apartment with them. Fernande Olivier attests:*

Picasso is going crazy over Negro works and statues - masks and fetishes from all the countries of Africa are accumulating at his place. 1910.

Picasso considered [214]*those masks were not just pieces of sculpture like the rest. Not in the least, they were magic. The Negroes were intercessors. Their art was exorcising.*

He received great fame, for reproducing the very art by which Africans were judged inferior.

In the early 18th century slave traders captured West African native, Job ben Solomon and sold him into slavery. Solomon provides the best evidence of the education of West Africans. He had memorized the entire Koran and managed to convince his captors to release him. Job is just one example of the many [215]*Petitions by free people of color who were captured and sent into slavery.*

---

[213] Gandhi: The Traditional Roots of Charisma, Susanne Hoeber Rudolph, Lloyd I. Rudolph, University of Chicago Press, 1983 pg.32

[214214] Picasso: A Biography By Patrick O'Brian W. W. Norton & Company, Mar 17, 1994 pg.154

[215] Journal of the House of Representatives of the United States/ United States. Congress. House Francis Childs and John Swain, 1816 81.

In 1871 Carl Mauch, visited the ruins of an old city in Zimbabwe and found tightly fitted granite about 32 feet high and 17 feet thick the locals called it mumbahru (house of the great woman).

[216] The town is believed to have been built and occupied during the reign of the Axum Empire, from the 5th through the 15th century. It has very similar construction to medieval Scottish villages.

This ruined city has a great tower in the enclosure, which may have been a temple.

[217]Albert Churchward a prominent freemason in the mid-20th century, described the connections between Africans, Mexicans and the Egyptians. He considered the Africans of Great Zimbabwe, as the ancient Egyptians who called themselves, *Makalanga* the *children of the sun.*

Figure 90 Great Zimbabwe by Dr.LyleConrad

Figure 91 12-13th century Nigerian Brass Warriors in shining armor Edo, Court of Benin; image by Michel wal

Nazi archaeologists and anthropologists Heinrich Himmler and Leo Frobenius head of German Inter African Exploration in the early 1900's set out to Africa to find evidence for the theory of white supremacy. They were among the architects of the developing world's perceptions about Africa. Frobenius declared, after seeing sculptures in Ife, Nigeria. 1910:

Here were the remains of a very ancient and fine type of art, infinitely nobler than the comparatively coarse stone images, not even well preserved. These meager relics were eloquent of a symmetry, a vitality, a delicacy of form <u>directly reminiscent of ancient Greece</u> and a proof that once upon a time, <u>a race far superior in strain to the Negro, had been settled here.</u>

[218]*Among the rich artistic traditions of the Guinea coast, we focus here on ancient Ife (also known as Ile-Ife), the cradle of contemporary Yoruba culture. Situated in the West African forest, Ife was the center of a trading network that capitalized on its accessibility from the Niger and several smaller rivers, from the West African coast, and from the savanna country to the north. Stone monoliths are characteristic of early Ife art, while in the latter half of the first millennium A.D. distinct styles of finely modeled terracotta representations and works in cast metal were refined. This period is also significant for the emergence of lost-wax casting. While the smelting of metallic ores dates to the first millennium B.C., and by about 1000 A.D. iron and copper smelting techniques had spread throughout the continent.*

---

[216]Mysteries of History by Robert Stewart PHD with Clint Twist and Edward Horton. A National Geographic Project
[217] The signs and symbols of primordial man :4bthe evolution of religious ... By Albert Churchward
[218] http://www.metmuseum.org/toah/hd/wax/hd_wax.htm

[219]Iron use, in smelting and forging for tools, appears in Nok culture in West Africa at least by 1000 BC and possibly earlier. There is inescapable evidence of African development much earlier than their European counterparts.

After traversing the world and finally reading all the writings of history it became clear that there truly was no evidence for white supremacy. What we understand as world wars, were simply measures to destroy these records and historical artifacts around the world. [220]*The Nazi conspirators destroyed 1,670 Greek Orthodox Churches, 237 Roman Catholic Churches, 67 Chapels, 427 museums and many thousands of residential buildings: they removed 10,000 works of art:* and attempted to erase every indication of a Jewish or African presence in Europe and the world. It is quite possible that many of the paintings were altered. The estate of Tolstoy, Pushkin and other famous poets and writers were sacked and today this destruction continues.

What we can determine from our study of history, is that there was great disunity among the African nations. This appears from the many names given to them as distinct groups. For this reason, slaves were actually sold to Europeans by their African brothers, just like joseph was.

Those who were sold into slavery were not always the subservient and uneducated castes. Many of the prosperous nations and peoples were taken captive and sent away to ensure the safe governing of the usurping regime.

Leo Africanus tells us of iron and gold mines and every mark of advancement. Merchants came from around the world to trade with the Africans.

---

[219] Duncan E. Miller and N.J. Van Der Merwe, 'Early Metal Working in Sub Saharan Africa' Journal of African History 35 (1994) 1-36
Minze Stuiver and N.J. Van Der Merwe, 'Radiocarbon Chronology of the Iron Age in Sub-Saharan Africa' Current Anthropology 1968. Tylecote 1975
[220] Nazi Conspiracy and Aggression, (Volume 4) United States. Office of Chief of Counsel for the Prosecution of Axis Criminality U.S. Government Printing Office, 1946

about fortie miles distant from Niger. The kingdome of Guber[13] is enuironed with high mountaines, and containeth many villages inhabited by shepherds, and other herdsmen. Abundance of cattell here are both great and small : but of a lower stature then the cattell in other places. Heere are also great store of artificers and linnen weauers : and heere are such shooes[14] made as the ancient Romans were woont to weare, the greatest part whereof be carried to Tombuto and Gago. Likewise heere is abundance of rice, and of certaine other graine and pulse, the like whereof I neuer saw in Italie. In this region there is a certaine great village containing almost sixe thousand families, being inhabited with all kinde of merchants, and here was in times past the court of a certaine king, who in my time was slaine by *Ischia* the king of Tombuto, and Afterward he sent gouernours hither who mightily oppressed and impouerished the people that were before rich : and most part of the inhabitants were carried captiue and kept for slaues by the said *Ischia*.

Their education was also very selective, so that Negros like Job were probably part of a more affluent caste. The educated among the African people kept the rest of their people in darkness, thus keeping their fellow countrymen in perpetual bondage. These secrets as they were termed in the days of Aristotle, were various degrees of knowledge which have been guarded from the beginning of time. This is the reason why, all Africans do not all share the same stories. A unified African identity was only created by American prejudice. Those who have continued from one generation to another are according to Nostradamus, not the common and unlearned crowd of idiot astrologers and Barbarians, but *priests for the rite*. Part of the royal priesthood, which have been dispersed among all the nations; and sown there as *wheat among tares* or *sheep among wolves*.

Hippolyto Joseph da Costa (1774-1823), a Brazilian author and one of the founders of the modern Freemasons, explains that the *mysteries were concealed from the vulgars; because it would be a ridiculous prostitution of such sublime theories to disclose them to the multitude incapable of understanding them, when even many of the initiates, did not comprehend the whole meaning of the symbols.*

These secret societies, were established to ensure that the leadership of the world would always tilt according to Providence; but by the mid-1800s precisely the age of Darwin

[221] *In France the tone of masonry was low. Admissions were sold at a fixed price without inquiry as to character.*

Pope Leo XII mourned over the corruption of the universities. In his Quo Graviora, of 1826, Education became the open door to an underground revolution. Everything from the history of the Earth to the history of nations was being rewritten.

The new societies although intriguing to the outsider, derive power solely from their membership. They are highly selective of promising, scholars. This ensures that the tiny percentage of the wealthiest people in the world continue to control it. But they operate on a flawed ideology and have no divine connection. They can only follow the very same prophecies which have been made available to all of us. This is the primary reason why the reading of the book is greatly discouraged. The very same education which the founding fathers and the builders of nations, science and industries have credited for their genius, has been separated from the education of their youth:

So we wrestle not against flesh and blood, but against ideology, *principalities, against powers, against the rulers of the darkness of this age, against spiritual wickedness in high places.* Ephesians 6:12

The facts begin to unravel the old theories of racial superiority; but a modern version of the theory now connects the advances of African Americans to *European* admixture. DNA analysis of African Americans reveal 20 to 35 percent European specific genes; so what exactly is European and who is mixed with who? The idea of a pure race is a search for Tacitus' vision of the Northerners, and this is the reasoning behind "ethnic cleansing" and why millions of people were killed and removed from their homes. There is no longer a pure race; we are all a mix-up of people. If we were to seriously consider the one drop rule, then there are almost no *white* people left. Most European people today are probably the most recent descendants of Africans. Thus they embody the stories of many civilizations, races and languages. This is why we do not find a universal feature among Europeans.

Many of us have a lineage of both vandals and civilians, on one side we may be crying the tears of Anne Frank, but on the other inflicting the pain of Hitler. On one end we are masters of slaves, but on the other end we are the slaves. Our backgrounds are more than race. Each of us now have many stories all rolled in one, so there is no one to whom we can direct our anger. We are forced to learn the language of love.

The poison with which the enemy tries to destroy you is one which has nearly killed him. This argument of assigning an admixture to genius unravels the controversy of racial superiority right where it started, amongst the blondes once considered "dumb blondes" and the blackheads, in Europe. We can clearly see how the spirit selects the most unlikely candidates. It is precisely because of David's inferiority we look for the force behind his success over the mighty Goliath. The Northern raiders, without homes or even the knowledge to build are now the engineers, the Africans once associated with wisdom, wealth and prestige, become the lowest of all people. Everything turns upside down.

---

[221] Encyclopædia Britannica: A-ZYM Day Otis Kellogg, Thomas Spencer Baynes, William Robertson Smith Werner, 1903 volume(F)Freemasonry pg750

Today the European man takes the place of divinity in Nefertari's stead. The stories revolve and the Earth simply recycles the same stories. We now know that one of the greatest scientists to have lived was Newton, a Blonde haired man, and the most notorious evil was committed by Hitler a dark haired man and probably a Jew.

In 1957 the sun gradually begun to rise again and 1963 Dr. Martin Luther King had a dream. He spoke this dream as if into existence, so that today we are judged by our character and not our appearance. We have come this far so that we can examine the contrast between the divinity of the Egyptians and now Europeans, both connected to skin color. It seems obvious that our mixed nation was designed to eliminate any correlation between color and intelligence.

If we don't accept this fact, then the United States of America will go the way of all other empires in history. This is our impasse; a thousand years of peace or the next exodus.

The ladder of racial superiority now looks more like a spinning round table. The more advanced and civilized, now have the responsibility and mission, to provide the same salvation, grace and mercy which was before extended to them to save the new backward, heathens of the world.

Every living thing loses color, it's not an evolutionary accomplishment, this is the genius of our design. Variety is the spice, and if the whole world lost its color, there would be no way to color it again.

Figure 92. A)AlejandroLinares Garcia –LizardZipolite, b) Ocellated_Lizards_ Jason Pratt&bkimmel-c)-Nevit Dilmen-white Peacock_00788, e)-Snowflake gorilla-Barcelona Zoo-Bearpark-1 f) black gorilla-Barcelona Zoo-Bearpark

The ancient spirit is not restricted to any particular race. The ancient spirit is a persona, it is especially revealed in our ability to cry, in our culture, and ideology of one love. It is a particular aura, embodied. Those who possess it look up. Bacon defined it, as a *Depth and compass and largest most universal understanding.*

The world of racial division must end, because there is no more black or white, we can finally be united.

We begin the story where it ended. The first is now the last, the beginning is now the end. The Ethiopians have been training for this race from the beginning. They had to learn to develop a meek and patient spirit. The prophet Jeremiah (12:5) says that they were trained to outrun the horses. Isaiah also promised that:

They that wait upon the Lord shall renew their strength; they shall mount up with wings as eagles; they shall run, and not be weary; and they shall walk, and not faint. 40:31

Today a new direction is once again met with opposition, as a new leader comes in riding on the Democratic Party's donkey.

Moreover he led them in the day by a cloudy pillar; and in the night by a pillar of fire, to give them light in the way that they should go. Nehemiah 9:12

This sign led the children of Israel to freedom across the red sea. It Led Rome against the pagans and heathens, and America to liberty from the British; and it appeared again before the 2012 U.S. election of President Barak Obama. Just a few days before the election, Americans were stuck in the desert between a return to bondage and the Promised Land. Then in the *Sandy* desert, appeared a storm like it did so many times before. Over the pillar of fire, symbolically raised by Liberty's hand, a mighty cloud of Providential guidance appeared. President Obama is now called to expel the new atheistic priesthood and to establish the next phase of Earth's maturity.

The moon's reign has passed, the sun takes up his remaining days.

The prophecies and warnings of Nostradamus are now accomplished.

We can now awake from the short night of the underworld. Providence is finally revealed and a new kingdom rises, with a bound of men whose identities are forged in their common destiny; united in whom they believe even when divided by what it is they do.

Until the philosophy which holds one race superior and another Inferior Is finally, and permanently, discredited and abandoned - Everywhere will be war ....Bob Marley

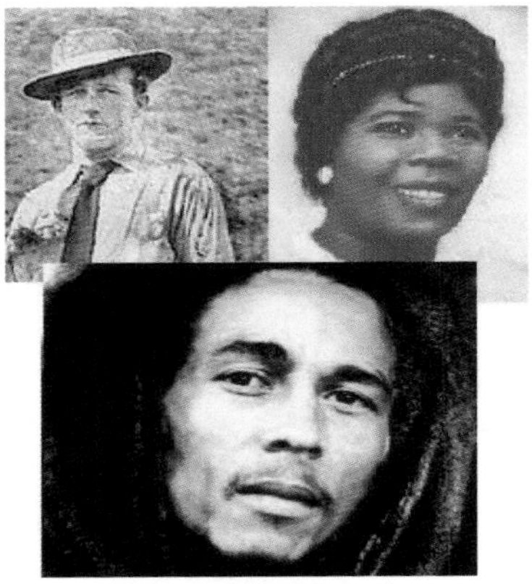

Figure 93 Legendary Jamaican Artist Bob Marley & his parents Norval & Cedella Marley

The goal set before us is the completion of the pyramid of Knowledge.

This pyramid does not require our hands but the love and unity of our minds through the *All Seeing Eye.*

The atheists have organized crusades to rewrite the beginning of the book. By doing so, they hope to change the end of the story; but they will not retain their dominion over the world; because the book has compensated for the rewrites.

A Promise left behind for the Ethiopian People

The Ethiopian woman represents Tiye and a wife rejected by her husband.
Jesus prophesized that:

> The *Queen of the South* will rise at the end with the people of this generation and condemn them Luke 11:31

> According to the old Egyptian legend Isis must put all the pieces of her dead husband back together to initiate the resurrection.

> *Joel 2:18-32*

> This woman according to Revelations 12 was *a woman clothed with the Sun*. Who battles the mighty serpent.

> She cries: *I am black, but beautiful [too], O ye daughters of Jerusalem,* [223] *as the tents of Kedar,*

Look not upon me, because I am black, because *the sun hath looked upon me:* my mother's children were angry with me; they made me the keeper of their vineyards; But mine own vineyard I have not kept.

Songs of Solomon 1:5-6

She will reap the harvest, which he has promised her. Hezekiah Walker

The second part of the book of Isaiah seems to be dedicated to her instruction. It spoke patience into her DNA. As a queen who has lost all glory and honor. Isaiah 54

2 Enlarge the place of thy tent, and let them stretch forth the curtains of thine habitations: spare not, lengthen thy cords, and strengthen thy stakes;

3 For thou shalt break forth on the right hand and on the left; and thy seed shall inherit the Gentiles, and make the desolate cities to be inhabited.

4 Fear not; for thou shalt not be ashamed: neither be thou confounded; for thou shalt not be put to shame: for thou shalt forget the shame of thy youth, and shalt not remember the reproach of thy widowhood any more.

---

[222] Regarded as powerful expressions of nobility and dignity, these sculptures proved to be highly popular: casts were acquired by the Museum of National History in Paris and also by Queen Victoria. The Walters' pair were cast by the Paris foundry Eck and Durand in 1852. These bronzes were esteemed by 19th-century viewers as expressions of human pride and dignity in the face of grave injustice. *Walters Art Museum 1851*

[223] Observations on divers passages of Scripture. Placing many of them in a light altogether new ... and more amply illustrating the rest than has been yet done, by means of circumstances incidentally mentioned in books of voyages and travels into the East in two volumes.Thomas Harmer, Sir John Chardin, Printed for J. Johnson, 1797

[*Arabs retain the most ancient customs of using Black goats-hair on their tents. The present distinction however appears by this passage to have been as ancient as the days of Solomon.*]Pg. 139

5 For thy Maker is thine husband (once more you will be his wife); the Lord of hosts is his name; and thy Redeemer the Holy One of Israel; The God of the whole earth shall he be called.

6 For the Lord hath called thee as a woman forsaken and grieved in spirit, and a wife of youth, when thou was refused, saith thy God.

7 For <u>a small moment</u> have I forsaken thee; but with great mercies will I gather thee.

8 In a little wrath I hid my face from thee for a moment; but with everlasting kindness will I have mercy on thee, saith the Lord thy Redeemer.

9 For this is as the waters of Noah unto me: for as I have sworn that the waters of Noah should no more go over the earth; so have I sworn that I would not be wroth with thee, nor rebuke thee.

10 For the mountains shall depart, and the hills be removed; but my kindness shall not depart from thee, neither shall the covenant of my peace be removed, saith the Lord that hath mercy on thee.

11 O thou afflicted, tossed with tempest, and not comforted, behold, I will lay thy stones with fair colors, and lay thy foundations with sapphires.

12 And I will make thy windows of agates, and thy gates of carbuncles, and all thy borders of pleasant stones.

13 And all thy children shall be taught of the Lord; and great shall be the peace of thy children.

14 In righteousness shalt thou be established: thou shalt be far from oppression; for thou shalt not fear: and from terror; for it shall not come near thee.

15 Behold, they shall surely gather together, but not by me: whosoever shall gather together against thee shall fall for thy sake.

16 Behold, I have created the [224]smith that bloweth the coals in the fire, and that bringeth forth an instrument for his work; and I have created the waster to destroy.

[All of your suffering has been divinely appointed, but this time]

17 <u>No weapon that is formed against you shall prosper;</u> and every tongue that shall rise against you in judgment you shalt condemn.

This is the heritage of the servants of the Lord, and their righteousness is of me, saith the Lord.

Isaiah 52

Awake, awake; put on thy strength, O Zion; put on thy beautiful garments, O Jerusalem, the holy city: for henceforth there shall no more come into thee the uncircumcised and the unclean.

2 Shake thyself from the dust; arise, and sit down, O Jerusalem: loose thyself from the bands of thy neck, O captive daughter of Zion.

4 For thus saith the Lord God, My people went down before time into Egypt to sojourn there; and the Assyrian oppressed them without cause.

8 Thy watchmen shall lift up the voice; with the voice together shall they sing: for they shall see eye to eye, when the Lord shall bring again Zion.

9 Break forth into joy, sing together, ye waste places of Jerusalem: for the Lord hath comforted his people, he hath redeemed Jerusalem.

10 The Lord hath made bare his holy arm in the eyes of all the nations; and all the ends of the earth shall see the salvation of our God.

---

[224] German "smithaz" meaning "skilled worker

11 Depart ye, depart ye, go ye out from thence, touch no unclean thing; go ye out of the midst of her; be ye clean, that bear the vessels of the Lord.

12 For ye shall not go out with haste, nor go by flight: for the Lord will go before you; and the God of Israel will be your reward.

13 Behold, my servant shall deal prudently, he shall be exalted and extolled, and be very high.

14 As many were astonished at thee; his face was so marred more than any man, and his form more than the sons of men:

Figure 94 Henri Béchard (The Sphinx Armachis, Cairo), about 1880.

15 So shall he sprinkle many nations; the kings shall shut their mouths at him: For that which had not been told them they shall now see; and that which they had not heard shall they now consider.

Isaiah 61

The Spirit of the Lord God is upon me; because the Lord hath anointed me to preach good tidings unto the meek; he hath sent me to bind up the brokenhearted, to proclaim liberty to the captives, and the opening of the prison to them that are bound;

2 To proclaim the acceptable year of the Lord, and the day of vengeance of our God; to comfort all that mourn;

3 To appoint unto them that mourn in Zion, to give unto them beauty for ashes, the oil of joy for mourning, the garment of praise for the spirit of heaviness; that they might be called trees of righteousness, the planting of the Lord, that he might be glorified.

4 And they shall build the old wastes, they shall raise up the former desolations, and they shall repair the waste cities, the desolations of many generations.

5 And strangers shall stand and feed your flocks, and the sons of the alien shall be your plowmen and your vinedressers.

6 But ye shall be named the Priests of the Lord: men shall call you the Ministers of our God: ye shall eat the riches of the Gentiles, and in their glory shall ye boast yourselves.

7 For your shame ye shall have double; and for confusion they shall rejoice in their portion: therefore in their land they shall possess the double: everlasting joy shall be unto them.

8 For I the Lord Love judgment, I hate robbery for burnt offering; and I will direct their work in truth, and I will make an everlasting covenant with them.

9 And their seed shall be known among the Gentiles, and their offspring among the people: all that see them shall acknowledge them, that they are the seed which the Lord hath blessed.

Hebrews 11

By faith Abraham, when he was called to go out into a place which he should after receive for an inheritance, obeyed; and he went out, not knowing whither he went.

By faith he sojourned in the land of promise, as in a strange country, dwelling in tabernacles with Isaac and Jacob, the heirs with him of the same promise:

By faith Moses, choose to suffer affliction with the people of God, than to enjoy the pleasures of sin for a season;

And what shall I more say? For the time would fail me to tell of Gideon, and of Barak, and of Samson, and of Jephthae; of David also, and Samuel, and of the prophets:

> And in this age of the Europeans who accepted the promises by faith and left darkness and heathenism and carried the torch to save the world or the Ethiopians removed from their homeland and led into slavery but held on to the promise which they traded for their glory, that by faith they would not be ashamed forever.

> The Jews who continued to call *aba* to the father who seemed to have deserted them.

> By faith, Native Americans prepared the land for all the people of the world. Whereby a remnant of their seed would be reserved. Finally the Asians traded a major role in the story for nirvana, and today they are the most populous people of the world.

33 (Those kings) who through faith subdued kingdoms, wrought righteousness, obtained promises, stopped the mouths of lions.

34 Quenched the violence of fire, escaped the edge of the sword, out of weakness were made strong, waxed valiant in fight, turned to flight the armies of the aliens.

35 Women received their dead raised to life again: and others were tortured, not accepting deliverance; that they might obtain a better resurrection:

36 And others had trial of cruel mockings and scourgings, yea, moreover of bonds and imprisonment:

37 They were stoned, they were sawn asunder, were tempted, and were slain with the sword: they wandered about in sheepskins and goatskins; being destitute, afflicted, tormented;

38 (Of whom the world was not worthy :) they wandered in deserts, and in mountains, and in dens and caves of the earth.

39 And these all, having obtained a good report through faith, received not the promise:

40 God having provided some better thing for us, that they without us could not be made perfect.

> But now we are all here, we are all awake and conscious of the continuity of the Gospel and the purpose and design of God.

> When we study the history of the world as random and isolated events we fail to see the big picture. In fact all of our studies have failed to produce the same imagery and connection as the ancients who carried little more than these stories.

> We have moved from the metaphoric brain to a highly mechanical one. An age of minds overloaded with irrelevant information, and disconnected from reality of our true story. When we continue the story by adding the pieces of our own time to the ancient quilt, it appears now as a massive mosaic. Purpose and reason animate our stories and transforms them from a combination of events and a collection of facts, to a

live performance infused with spirit, personality, love, hope, fear, anger, disobedience, resentment, appreciation and trust.

How can we tell the history without the character of Providence? This force which so many leaders have intimately connected to and called upon. We cannot forget Jonah's obstinacy, Tirhakah's cries, Senecribe's pride, Hezekiah's humility, Nebucandezzar's insanity, Croesus' stupidity, Alexander's claim to divinity, Caracalla's cruelty, Charlemagne's majesty, Washington's appreciation, or Barak's revolution. Together we see the grand design, as this story ends and a new Earth is prepared to be born.

Romans 11:23 and if they do not persist in unbelief, they will be grafted in, for God is able to graft them in again.

Isaiah 25:8 he will swallow up death forever. The Sovereign LORD will wipe away the tears from all faces; he will remove the disgrace of his people from all the earth. The LORD has spoken.

As He says also in Hosea:

For He will finish the work and cut it short in righteousness,
because the LORD will make a short work upon the earth.

We are still at war, those soldiers who survive won't be the bravest or the strongest. They won't be the most righteous. The survivors will be those who follow the commands of the most efficient captain of all time.

And the seventh angel sounded; and there were great voices in heaven, saying, the kingdoms of this world are become the kingdoms of our Lord, and of his Christ; and he shall reign forever and ever. Revelation 11:15

The Seventh Millennium

I saw Zion in a vision Jah was there amidst everyone, stretching forth his right hand, oh it's like a family reunion. Garnet Silk

This is the last exodus. What was before I cannot say, but I only know that I am here. The city has no need of the sun, neither of the moon, to shine in it: for the glory of God lightens it, and the Lamb is the light thereof. Revelation 21:23

There are millions of us. The first person I see is my daughter, she died at the age of three and I have been longing to hold her again ever since.

Sister Claire from my old convent is shocked to see so many of her naughty girls here and so few of her sisters.

Off in the distance some very unexpected people are here, it seems like everyone is having a party, the most interesting people who ever lived are all here. We even have the star of Rambo. Everyone is exchanging their story of how they overcame.

The angels are hosting a reception in our honor, they have been waiting on us as if we were dignitaries.

Time was condensed so we don't have to walk or fly, we can just decide where we want to be and we are there instantly. The Children are all over the place, because it is safe to explore here.

There is a sense of timelessness here, the trees are continually bearing 12 fruits per tree. The fruits don't fall off to the ground, once picked a new fruit appears in place, because the cycles of growth and death have all been changed. There are museums of literal eras in time here, so I can visit Tiye in Egypt; and whisper words of consolation to her; "awesome"! Now it makes sense why God never spoke at length, everyone in reality, is too busy to stop and listen, so we've learnt to use the recorded words like *be still* or *I am with you*. It's so amazing how effective those words are.

Besides the streets of gold and the massive mansions, and the breathtaking views, the greatest part is the feeling. It is the high that the addict chases an ecstasy that does not fade away, a consistent equilibrium of happiness and peace.

No one has seen the father, we are told that he is building new Earths and we will all have the honor to blow in the breath of life and to meet the new Adams.

And we shall see his face; and his name shall be in our foreheads.

And he said unto me, these sayings are faithful and true: and the Lord God of the holy prophets sent his angel to shew unto his servants the things which must shortly be done. Revelation 22:4-6

Micah 4

1 But in the last days it shall come to pass, that the mountain of the house of the Lord shall be established in the top of the mountains, and it shall be exalted above the hills; and people shall flow unto it.

2 And many nations shall come, and say, Come, and let us go up to the mountain of the Lord, and to the house of the God of Jacob; and he will teach us of his ways, and we will walk in his paths: for the law shall go forth of Zion, and the word of the Lord from Jerusalem.

3 And he shall judge among many people, and rebuke strong nations afar off; and they shall beat their swords into plowshares, and their spears into pruning hooks: nation shall not lift up a sword against nation, neither shall they learn war any more.

4 But they shall sit every man under his vine and under his fig tree; and none shall make them afraid: for the mouth of the Lord of hosts hath spoken it.

5 For all people will walk everyone in the name of his god, and we will walk in the name of the Lord our God for ever and ever.

6 In that day, saith the Lord, will I assemble her that halteth, and I will gather her that is driven out, and her that I have afflicted;

7 And I will make her that halted a remnant, and her that was cast far off a strong nation: and the Lord shall reign over them in mount Zion from henceforth, even forever.

History

When we study the reign of Kings and leaders through the millennias from Djoser to Obama, we can find many patterns, which coalesce into golden rules of leadership. Each leader is crowned under a divine mission or mandate which is clearly given as a beacon for his days in office. His success can only be evaluated many years after his term if the seeds he plants materialize. The role and weight of Providence in the success and demise of kings is also revealed through the prayers or self-reliance of each leader. Historians, prophets and scribes are employed in every generation to chronicle this unique relationship between Providence and the prosperity or destruction of nations. The greater mission is outlined as bringing the world out of darkness and into a unified consensus to follow this divine lead.

- Examine Croesus and Taharqa both kings sought out divine help, but had different outcomes.
- Necho's divine warrant opposed to Josiah's righteousness.
- The prosperity of the 18th Dynasty as a probable precursor for ignoring the ancient prophecies.
- Compare and contrast the reign and prayers of leaders like Taharqa and Josiah, both righteous men with very different outcomes.
- Hezekiah and Constantine, both inadvertently invited the enemy to take over their kingdoms.
- Necho and Cyrus, both operating on divine orders.
- Nebuchadnezzar and Alexander, became proud. (Pride comes before the fall)
- Compare Clovis, Athelstan, Charlemagne, Mansa Musa and George Washington, all of these men received an ideology as the foundation of their nations, but the nations which received Christianity grew while Musa's wealthy Kingdom fell.
- Compare Leo Africanus' survey of Africa as it led to the takeover of the continent by European colonialists and the modern day treason of U.S. employee Snowden who fled to Russia with extremely significant US intelligence.

Consider the consistent correlation of natural disasters and plagues to the down fall of Kingdoms. Research the extent to which these disasters have aided in politics and war and determine the extent to which the prayers of Kings and leaders can be said to have been answered.

Compare the world Before Christ to the world After his Departure:

- How did Jesus save the world?
  (In terms of laws and ethics) What would the world have been like without the development of a Christian creed of theology?

- Why did Paul deter the Galatians from following some of the laws and traditions of the Jews? Acts 15
- Why was the Jewish faith and the Muslim faith which were built on the same laws as the Christian faith determined ineffective? Or how could they have been?

Joseph Kraus Kopf's book titled *The Jews and Moors in Spain* M. Berkowitz & Company, 1886, is an excellent resource for the reasoning and historical context for the development of Islam.

When we study the anthropological descriptions of past cultures and societies we discover many connections to the present day.

- Research the extent to which education and theology actually transforms a culture in the debate of *nurture vs. nature*. Determine whether education has the power to actually cause a complete transformation or does it accentuate the innate culture of the people.
- In Europe you could draw connections between the ancient Scythians like the atheists who only believed in what they could observe, despised all other races and were notorious for defacing or destroying and taking over other established civilizations. The Gaul's also sacrificed people to burn like the new Christian converts did to accused witches.
- In Asia, Asians sought separation and isolation, while some Africans were wild and untamable, others pious submissive subjects willing to be controlled and led like lambs to slaughter.
- Africans in general emphasize the afterlife and many still feast in times of mourning in *going home* ceremonies.
- Is there a connection between African reverence of the mother over the father and the Roman Catholic tradition where Mary is venerated as an important figure?
- Is there a connection between the many reports of the ancient family structure among Africans in which Fathers play almost no role in rearing children, and modern African American families where many fathers are absent.

Research how these differences may have been used to determine the prophetic direction that the world would take.

In the study of language show how the diversity and change in a population is reflected in changes to language. This can also be used to study genetics.

- If all languages from Latin to English can be shown to have had external influences on their development, how does this explain the origin of the first language?
- Does the recognition of nakedness suggest that they are among people who are clothed, like the angels described by the prophets?
- Show how the separation of languages described in the story of the tower of Babel was recently represented in the formation of the romance languages from their Latin root, and the Afrikaans language in Africa within the past three centuries.
- If language is tied to ethnic identity, then how does the death of the Latin language relate to the indigenous Italians? And if the same is true, how does the survival of European languages

like English among such vast ethnic groups, add credence to the hypothesis that the Moors heavily influenced the separation of these languages?

- Finally how does the *Tifinagh* script of the Tuareg people in the Southern Saharan region corroborate the early European observation that they were originally Egyptians?
- Then also what historical event may have triggered their diffusion from Egypt into West Africa? How does the subsequent end of the language in North Africa in the 7th Century after the Arabians moved in correlate to the current population?

The irony is that you would have to live as long as God does to see the big picture.

The book of Daniel is littered with an underlying tone of the changing faces and the idea of the old prophets losing their respect. It reveals a perplexing dilemma in the days of Jerimiah and Daniel as the people were now changing before their eyes and there is a variance between Daniel's reasoning and God's. God tells Daniel that the people will all become white and this he says is a purification, but how is this a purification Daniel wonders. He fasts and prays and when the angel attends him, he is bronze in skin as if out of a furnace. That story of walking out of the furnace and the contrasting theme of what is meant by purification (as Job eludes to) Daniel wonders if he is clean, and the angel assures him that he is most worthy; but this purification is not as the *passing through fire,* it will later become a cleansing through water, or baptism. There is no way to explain this to Daniel so the angel asks him to forget about it.

Historians, Chroniclers and Scribes

Homer author of the Iliad and the Odyssey, ancient Greek poet. 800BC

Hanno the Navigator was a Carthaginian explorer 500 BC, best known for his exploration to the West African coast. He held the throne as nominal king of Carthage from 480- 440 BC

Herodotus Greek historian born in Halicarnassus, Caria (modern day Bodrum, Turkey) 484–425 BC. Considered "The Father of History" first by Cicero), because he was the first historian known to make inquiry into the history of the world and to collect artifacts and test the accuracy of information.

Manethon or Manetho, was a 3rd century BC Egyptian historian and priest; and the only Egyptian priests to have composed the history of the country in Greek. He lived during the Ptolemaic era and authored Aegyptiaca (History of Egypt). Josephus provides one of the earliest surviving references to Manetho's Aegyptiaca in the chapter "Against Apion".

Berosos was a Babylonian writer, a priest of Bel Marduk who wrote the History of Chaldea in the Koine Greek language, and who was active at the beginning of the 3rd century BC.

Histories, which covered the period of 264–146 BC in detail.

Polybius 200–. 118 BC was a Greek historian of the Hellenistic Period noted for his work, The

Diodorus Siculus was a Greek ethnographer and historian, who wrote works of history from 60 to 30 BC. Author of Bibliotheca historica, an astounding library of observations, firsthand accounts and interviews of his day and inquiry into the histories of people from ancient times.

Moses (1200 BC)
Jonah 800 BC
Isaiah (740-698 BC)
Jeremiah 650-570 BC
Zephaniah prophesied during the reign of King Josiah (640–609 BC.)
Ezekiel 622-570 BC
Daniel 623 BC to-Mid 6thC.

Zechariah and Ezra (480–440 BC)

Joel 400-360 BC

Jesus 30AD
Paul 70 AD
Phillip 70 AD
Thaddeus 70 AD
Titus Flavius Josephus (37 – 100) was a Jewish scholar and historian, who was born in Jerusalem.

Quintus Septimius Florens Tertullianus, or Tertullian 160 – 225, was the first Christian writer of Latin Christian literature sometimes referred to as "the father of Latin Christianity."

Pliny the Elder or Gaius Plinius Secundus was a Roman historian from 23– 79 AD),

Saint Cyprian 200 – 258 the bishop of Carthage and the head bishop of the African Council of 87 members

Augustine of Hippo or Saint Augustine 354 – 430, was the bishop of Algeria in West Africa. His writings are considered to have laid the foundation of Western Philosophy.

Pliny's Natural History. In Thirty-seven Books, Volumes 1-3 Pliny (the Elder.)Club, 1848 - Natural history author of The Natural History an early encyclopedia published circa AD 77–79 by. One of the largest single works to have survived from the Roman Empire to the modern day and covers all ancient knowledge.

Tacitus, Publius/Gaius, Cornelius 56 - 117 AD senator and a historian of the Roman Empire

Lucian of Samosata (125 –180 AD) is filled with sarcasm and wit which are latent throughout his work awaiting an audience like that of our 21st century.

Plutarch of Athens (350 – 430 AD) was a Greek Philosopher.

Procopius of Caesarea was a prominent scholar from Palaestina Prima 500 –565 AD.

Joannes Leo Africanus, 1494 - 1554 was a Moorish diplomat and author who is best known for his book Descrittione dell'Africa (Description of Africa) describing the geography of North Africa. Which inadvertently laid the ground work for colonial invasions.

Noah Webster conducted extensive research into history, his books helped to transform American language and culture. He also founded the Connecticut Society for the Abolition of Slavery in 1791

Thomas Spencer Baynes, William Robertson Smith Werner, 20th century authors of the Encyclopædia Britannica: A-ZYM Day Otis Kellogg, 1903 volume (F)

Saint Jerome 347 –420 was a Latin Christian priest, confessor, theologian and historian.

John of Ephesus (507- 586 AD) was a leader of the 6th century Syriac-speaking Church, and one of the earliest and most important of historians who wrote in Syriac.

Index and Glossary of Terms

Ethnographic Portraits of Past civilizations

America's First Civilization Ancient peoples and places / ISSN 1462-4869 by Richard A. Diehl

An African Civilization of Late Antiquity. Edinburgh: University Press page 63 Taddesse Tamrat (1994). Review of Stuart Munro-Hay 'Aksum: The Journal of African History. Stuart Munro-Hay (1991).

An Universal History: From the Earliest Accounts to the Present Time, Volume 16 Princeton University George Sale, George Psalmanazar, Archibald Bower, George Shelvocke, John Campbell, John Swinton C. Bathurst, 1780

Ancient and Modern Britons: A Retrospect, Volume 1 By David MacRitchie K. Paul, Trench & Company, 1884

Ancient Laws of Cambria: Containing the Institutional Triads of Dyonwal Moelmud, Howel the Good... and the Hunting Laws of Wales, to which are Added the Historical Triads Or Britain. Translated from the Welsh, by William Probert. - London, William Probert, 1823

Cambridge Ancient History, by Iorwerth Eiddon Stephen Edwards, I. E. S. Edwards, C. J. Gadd, N. G. L. Hammond.

Cambridge Ancient History: Volume 12, The Crisis of Empire, AD 193-337

Civilization Or Barbarism: An Authentic Anthropology By Cheikh Anta Diop, Chicago Review Press, Apr 1, 1991

Earth and Its Inhabitants ...: West Africa Elisée Reclus, Ernest George Ravenstein, Augustus Henry Keane D. Appleton, 1892

Egyptian Archaeology, (A summation of the theories proposed by William Matthew Flinders Petrie) by Willeke Wendrich/ John Wiley & Sons, Sep 26, 2011

Encyclopædia Britannica: A-ZYM Day Otis Kellogg, Thomas Spencer Baynes, William Robertson Smith Werner, 1903 volume(F)Fezzan

Letters to a Young Gentleman Commencing His Education: To which is Subjoined a Brief History of the United States by Noah Webster Howe & Spalding, S. Converse, printer, 1823 received by Harvard college in 1879.

Signs and symbols of primordial man : the evolution of religious ... By Albert Churchward

Song of Roland: Done Into English, in the Original Measure Dutton, 1920

Source book of medieval history: documents illustrative of European life and institutions from the German invasion to the Renaissance by Frederic Austin 1907

They Came Before Columbus African Studies professor Ivan van Sertima of Rutgers University/Dr. Clarence Weiant (1897-1986)

Titus Livius Patavinus, by Giacomo Filippo Tomasini, Andreas Frisius, 1670

Travels in Syria and Egypt, During the Years 1783, 1784, & 1785, Volume 1 Constantin-François Volney R. Morison, 1801 NOW by Joel A. Freeman, Ph.D.

Travels to Discover the Source of the Nile, in the Years 1768, Volume 3 - by James Bruce 1813

Two Thousand Years of Gild Life: An Outline of the History and Development of the Gild System from Early Times, with Special Reference to Its Application to Trade and Industry; Together with a Full Account of the Gilds and Trading Companies of Kingston-upon-Hull, from the 14th to the 18th Century Joseph Malet Lambert A. Brown and sons; [etc., etc.,], 1891 - Guilds – pg154

Voyage of Hanno: Translated, and Accompanied with the Greek Text, Explained from the Accounts of Modern Travellers, Defended Against the Objections of Mr. Dodwell and Other Writers, and Illustrated by Maps from Ptolemy, D'Anville, and Bougainville Hanno, Thomas Falconer by T. Cadell Jun. and Davies, 1797

Western Society: A Brief History, Volume 1: From Antiquity to Enlightenment. Page 50-51 John P. McKay, Bennett D. Hill, John Buckler, Clare Haru Crowston, Merry E. Wiesner-Hanks Publisher Macmillan, 2010 ISBN 0312594283, 9780312594282

World of Rome: An Introduction to Roman Culture Peter V. Jones, Keith C. Sidwell, Cambridge University Press, Mar 6, 1997

African Portraits

Some of the vast collection of portraits of Africa are catalogued in Georges Jules Victor Clairin,
Shepp's Library of History and Art: A Pictorial History of All Lands and Times; the Great Incidents of History Set Forth by the Magic Pencils of the World's Greatest Artists Daniel B. Shepp Globe Bible Publishing Company, 1905
And History painters Evelyn Brooks Higginbotham, Leon F. Litwack, Darlene Clark Hine
Harvard University Press, 2001

Kingdoms and Kings
Anabasis of Alexander, Or, The History of the Wars and Conquests of Alexander the Great
Arrian Hodder and Stoughton, 1884 – Iran bk1.

Ancient Egyptian Materials and Technology edited by Paul T. Nicholson, Ian Shaw

Ancient India as Described by Ptolemy: Being a Translation of the Chapters which Describe India and Central and Eastern Asia in the Treatise on Geography Written by Klaudios Ptolemaios, the Celebrated Astronomer: with Introduction, Commentary, Map of India According to Ptolemy, and a Very Copious Index by Ptolemy, John Watson McCrindle Thacker, Spink, & Company, 1885

Ancient state of Britain. Bedforshire – Essex Thomas Cox, Anthony Hall, Robert Morden 1738.

Apologies of Justin Martyr, Tertullian, and Minutius Felix: In Defence of the Christian Religion, with the Commonitory of Vincentius Lirinensis, Concerning the Primitive Rule of Faith, Translated from Their Originals: with Notes...and a Preliminary Discourse Upon Each Author. by William Reeves W.B., 1709

Christopher Columbus: His Life, His Works, His Remains: As Revealed by Original Printed and Manuscript Records, with an Essay on Peter Martyr of Anghera and Bartolomé de Las Casas, the First Historians of America, Volume 1

Daily Life Of The Nubians Robert Steven Bianchi

Early Dynastic Cemeteries of Naga-ed-Dêr, Volume 2 University of California. Hearst Egyptian Expedition, George Andrew Reisner, Arthur Cruttenden Mace, Albert Morton Lythgoe, Dows Dunham Hinrichs, 1908 - Naga-ed-Dêr

European traditions in the study of religion in Africa. By Frieder Ludwig, Afeosemime Unuose Adogame, Ulrich Berner, Christoph Bochinger, African Association for the Study of Religions.

From the beginning until the death of Alexander I Simon Dubnow, Jewish Publication Society of America, 1916

Gandhi: The Traditional Roots of Charisma, Susanne Hoeber Rudolph, Lloyd I. Rudolph, University of Chicago Press, Apr 15, 1983

Great Benin; Its Customs, Art and Horrors Henry Ling Roth Metro Books, 1903

Golden Age of the Moor by Ivan Van Sertima /Transaction Publishers, 1992

Great Captains: A Course of Six Lectures Showing the Influence on the Art of War of the Campaigns of Alexander, Hannibal, Cæsar, Gustavus Adolphus, Frederick, and Napoleon Theodore Ayrault Dodge Houghton Miffin, 1889

Library of Alexandria: Centre of Learning in the Ancient World, Revised Edition/ By Roy Malcolm MacLeod, Roy MacLeod I.B.Tauris.

Life of Alfred the Great Reinhold Pauli, Paulus Orosius, Benjamin Thorpe, G. Bell & sons, 1893 World history- 582

Norse Warfare: The Unconventional Battle Strategies of the Ancient Vikings by Martina Sprague

Notes and queries: a medium of communication for literary men, artists, antiquaries, genealogists, etc of 1859

Nubia and Abyssinia: comprehending their civil history, antiquities, arts, religion, literature, and natural history Michael Russell, J. & J. Harper, 1833 – Ethiopia

Search for Alexander. Little Brown & Co. Boston. Fox, Robin Lane (1980).

Travels Into the Inland Parts of Africa: Containing a Description of the Several Nations for the Space of Six Hundred Miles Up the River Gambia by Francis Moore Henry, 1738 (First hand account of Africa)

Ancient History (General)

Historical Library of Diodorus the Sicilian: In Fifteen Books. To which are Added the Fragments of Diodorus, and Those Published by H. Valesius, I. Rhodomannus, & F. Ursinus, translated by G Booth ESQ Harvard College Library In two volumes. Vol. 1 Diodorus Siculus.

History for Ready Reference: From the Best Historians, Biographers, and Specialists; Their Own Words in a Complete System of History (Josephus, Nelson, Larned, Alan, Campbell, Reiley) C.A. Nichols Company, 1895

History of Egypt: During the XVIIth and XVIIIth Dynasties. 1896, with Additions to 1898, Sir William Matthew Flinders Petrie, Charles Schribner's Sons, 1897

History of Herodotus, Volume 1 Herodotus Halicarnasseus, George Rawlinson, Henry Creswicke Rawlinson (sir), John Gardner Wilkinson (sir) J. Murray, 1862

History of Switzerland, from B.C. 110, to A.D. 1830 By Dionysius Lardner 1832

History of the conquest of Spain by the Arab-Moors: With a sketch of the civilization which they achieved, and imparted to Europe, Volume 2Henry Coppée, Little, Brown, 1881

In the Dictionary of Greek and Roman Geography, Volume 1 Sir William Smith in 1872 Extent and Population.

Jews and Moors in Spain by Joseph Krauskopf M. Berkowitz & Company, 1886. This is the best account of the history of Spain and the invasion from the records of Arabians and the comprehensive research of this author.

Journey-book of England. Berkshire (Derbyshire, Hampshire, Kent).By England 1840

Larcher's Notes on Herodotus: Historical and Critical Remarks on, Volume 1 By Pierre Henri Larcher 1829

New Larned History for Ready Reference, Reading and Research: The Actual Words of the World's Best Historians, Biographers and Specialists; a Complete System of History for All Uses, Extending to All Countries and Subjects and Representing the Better, Volume 1 Josephus Nelson Larned 1524- Page 273Verranzano's voyage along the Atlantic coast of North America.

New student's reference work a cyclopædia for teachers, students, and families, Volume 1

Nine Books of the History of Herodotus, Volume 2 by Henry Slatter, 1837

Oxford History of Ancient Egypt. Edited by Ian Shaw.

Periplus of the Erythraen Sea by a merchant of the First Century Hanno: a voyage of discovery down the West African coast Hanno Commercial Museum, 1913 Translated by Wilfred Schoff.

Pliny's natural History in thirty seven books. Translated from 1601 translation of Philemon Holland in 1847

Plutarch, page 276 Volume 4 by A. J. Valpy, 1832 by Plutarch

Race and the Writing of History : Riddling the Sphinx: Maghan Keita Assistant Professor of History and Director of Africana Studies Villanova University Social Science -Oxford University Press, 2000

Researches Into the Physical History of Mankind: In Two Volumes, Volume 1 by James Cowles Prichard 1826

Rethinking the Other in Antiquity Erich S. Gruen Princeton University Press, Aug 27, 2012

Second Book of History: Including the Modern History of Europe, Africa, and Asia : Designed as a Sequel to the First Book of History Samuel Griswold Goodrich Jenks, Hickling & Swan, 1852 page 114 referenced from Encyclopædia britannica: or, A dictionary of arts, sciences, and miscellaneous literature, Volume 17 Colin Macfarquhar, George Gleig A. Bell and C. Macfarquhar, 1797

World at War 1914-1939by Duncan Hill

Age of Adam

Geneticists use the male lineage represented by the bible as Adam and in science as the Y chromosome to trace our ancestry. To determine the age of Adam they apply a clock to the Y-chromosomes, which calculates the rate of mutations back to the beginning. The ability to determine the precise date when Y-chromosomal Adam lived depends on the accuracy and stability of this mutation rate. This method assumes that the current rate of mutation has remained constant from the beginning. But the bible tells us in Genesis 6:3 that this assumption is wrong:

Why? Because the rate of mutation has actually slowed down.

My spirit will no longer contend with man his life span will now be limited to 120 years.

If the scientific calculations are based on the modern mutation rate then this would drastically alter these results. The process of aging and dying that we are familiar with today only begun to take place generations after the initial creation. A new aging mutation like a form of Progeria was introduced in Adam's generation, this reduced the life span from an unlimited life span of immortality to an average of 806 years. Then in Noah's generation another mutation takes effect which fixed the maximum lifespan to what it is today, 120 years. (Genesis 6:2) In each subsequent generation, Adam is created in a *new image,* which represents a new mutation. *Adam also may not have encountered any mutations before Eden.*

When we adjust this average by the current upper limit of 120 years, it provides us with the same factor of 6.72 which we can use to synchronize the calculations. Thus Adam was born roughly 70,000/6.72 or 10416 (KYA). This was shortly after the end of the last glacial period and it coincides with the very rapid climate change at the beginning of Eden. (The calibration of this variance is thoroughly explained in the science volume under Genetics and virtually disappears in the context of an Earth age of 14± B.Y.)

Population Genetics

Journey of man: Wells, Spencer The A genetic odyssey. Princeton, NJ: Princeton University Press, 2002.

Living Races of Mankind. Hutchinson, London; 1, 5, reprinted in: Proc. roy. Soc. Med. Volume 67 February 1974.

Molecular Biology & Human Diversity. Anthony J. Boyce, C. G. Nicholas Mascie-Taylor Cambridge University Press

Y chromosomes traveling south: the cohen modal haplotype and the origins of the Lemba--the "Black Jews of Southern Africa". Thomas MG, Parfitt T, Weiss DA, Skorecki K, Wilson JF, le Roux M, Bradman N, Goldstein DB. The Center for Genetic Anthropology, Departments of Biology and Anthropology, University College London, London, United Kingdom. (Lemba Tribe of Africa)

(Tishkoff et al. 1996a, 1998a, 1998b; Calafell et al. 1998; Kidd et al. 1998) (Origin of Ethiopians)

The American Association of Physical Anthropologists meeting, held in Philadelphia, PA in March 2007 report by Ann Gibbons: European Skin Turned Pale Only Recently, Gene Suggests http://www.sciencemag.org/content/316/5823/364.1

Cornelia Di Gaetano,[1,10*] Nicoletta Cerutti,[1,10] Francesca Crobu,[1,11] Carlo Robino,[2] Serena Inturri,[2] Sarah Gino,[2] Simonetta Guarrera,[3] Peter A Underhill,[4] Roy J King,[5] Valentino Romano,[6] Francesco Cali,[7] Mauro Gasparini,[8] Giuseppe Matullo,[1,3] Alfredo Salerno,[9] Carlo Torre,[2] and Alberto Piazza[1]

Scriptural/ Religious Resources

Guns, Germs, and Steel: The Fates of Human Societies by Jared Diamond 1999

Handbook for Travellers in Northern Italy &c Murray, 1863

Historical atlas of the Bible by Dr. Ian Barnes

Kingdom of Priests: A History of Old Testament Israel Eugene H. Merrill, Baker Academic, Mar 1, 2008

Morgenthau, Henry (1918). Ambassador Morgenthau's Story. Garden City, New York: Doubleday.

Mycenaean Origin of Greek Mythology by Martin Persson Nilsson University of California Press, Jan 1, 1972

Mysteries of History by Robert Stewart PHD with Clint Twist and Edward Horton. A National Geographic Project

NAS Exhaustive Concordance of the Bible with Hebrew-Aramaic and Greek Dictionaries by The Lockman Foundation

National cyclopaedia - 1879

Natural Genesis: Or, Second Part of A Book of the Beginnings, Containing an Attempt to Recover and Reconstitute the Lost Origins of the Myths and Mysteries, Types and Symbols, Religion and Language, with Egypt for the Mouthpiece and Africa as the Birthplace, Volume 1 Gerald Massey Williams and Norgate, 1883

Art and Science

Picasso: A Biography By Patrick O'Brian W. W. Norton & Company, Mar 17, 1994

Religion and Science: Irreconcilable? A response to a greeting sent by the Liberal Ministers' Club of New York City. Published in The Christian Register, June, 1948. Crown Publishers, Inc., New York, 1954.

Image of Yasser Arafat Palestinian leader by Hans Jørn Storgaard Andersen

Source Hans Jørn Storgaard Andersen's personal video clip: http://wmedia.dk/index.php/Ha002.

Table of Figures.

Unless stated otherwise most images were derived from Wikipedia or free government sources.

Other Books from the Blue Prints for Life

Volume 2

The Science of Sacred Scripture is the complete integration of science philosophy and history. It reveals the scientific meanings of the ancient metaphors which have been passed down from generation to generation, with elementary simplicity. This is a universal code like an alphabet which uncovers the science of everything from biology, genetics and physics to love and sexuality, autism, death and dreams. This revolutionizes our ability to learn, acquire and store vast amounts of information through simple rules of universal order.

In Progress

Volume 3 in progress.

The Human Story reveals our purpose and the path we have to take to find it. The spirit is defined as a magnetic force which we begin to understand through science and the teachings of a diverse group of prophets. It cannot be yielded, because it is so much greater than any Earthly entity; but we can discover the methodology which makes us more attractive to this divine source. The anology used is your refridgerator. It cannot be moved by a tiny object, but you can discover how to make an object cling to the refridgerator. Many religions today concentrate on the color of the object, wether it is painted red or green. In this volume we discover how to become magnetic. We study how the power to be called sons of God requires a closer study of his teachings. This volume focuses on the actual Blue Print through many of the traditions and customs of our ancestors like head covering, removing shoes to enter a room and the purpose and power of prayer, fasting and other traditional practices.

Preview at theblueprintsforlife.org or thesoss.org

Made in the USA
Charleston, SC
29 March 2014